T0248270

ADVANCE PRAISE FOR
SUPPRESSING THE TRUTH IN DALLAS

"Brandt is more like an investigative reporter, going more in depth on his newest book on the JFK assassination."

—**Martin Scorsese**

SUPPRESSING THE TRUTH IN DALLAS

SUPPRESSING THE TRUTH IN DALLAS

CONSPIRACY, COVER-UP, AND INTERNATIONAL COMPLICATIONS IN THE JFK ASSASSINATION CASE

CHARLES BRANDT

Post Hill
PRESS

A POST HILL PRESS BOOK

Suppressing the Truth in Dallas:
Conspiracy, Cover-Up, and International Complications
in the JFK Assassination Case
© 2022 by Charles Brandt
All Rights Reserved

ISBN: 978-1-63758-315-9
ISBN (eBook): 978-1-63758-316-6

Cover design by Cody Corcoran
Interior design and composition by Greg Johnson, Textbook Perfect

Post Hill Press
New York • Nashville
posthillpress.com

Published in the United States of America
1 2 3 4 5 6 7 8 9 10

To Jenny Rose Brandt

Table of Contents

CHAPTER ONE

International Complications

On November 22, 1963, President John F. Kennedy's last breath was extinguished by a sniper's bullet in Dallas, Texas. Hidden from public view were the "international complications" behind the scenes.

Less than one day after assuming office, the new president, Lyndon Johnson, secretly began tape-recording telephone calls he made to government officials from the White House. One of his first calls was to prominent Republican Senator Everett Dirksen of Illinois. In his Texas drawl, Johnson confided to Dirksen: *"We got some international complications that could come up to us if we are not careful."*

This dire warning by the new president of a nuclear power in a Cold War setting was made while the rest of the world was sliding into a profound state of mourning.

These two powerful leaders, in attire appropriate for a presidential funeral, were plotting in concert. Johnson's warning to be "careful" had the quality of conspiracy. It was imperative enough to occupy their strategic thinking at a time like this. What they were up to has cried out to be chased down from its hiding place ever since.

These days, when government figures are exposed for lying, the media is inclined to bestow symbolic "Pinocchio" awards.

The race for Pinocchios is on. Please meet the contenders in order of wrongdoing:

1. Earl Warren, chief justice of the United States Supreme Court and President Johnson's appointee to chair the official investigation of the assassination of President Kennedy, the wounding of Texas Governor John Connally, and the murders of Dallas Police Officer J. D. Tippit and of President Kennedy's suspected assassin, Lee Harvey Oswald.

2. Jack Ruby, a Dallas strip club owner and close associate of Mafia figures. Ruby, who was intimate with crooked Dallas cops, shot and killed the assassination suspect Oswald in the Dallas Police Department basement two days after President Kennedy lost his life.

3. Melvin Belli was a prominent West Coast Mafia-connected trial lawyer. Three days after Ruby killed Oswald at the police station, Belli arrived in Dallas to take over with a secret legal plan to silence Ruby, who had just silenced Oswald. Whenever he won a case Belli fired a loud cannon blast on the roof of his San Francisco office building.

4. President Lyndon Johnson, who will be unmasked by his tape-recorded phone calls.

5. Attorney General Robert F. Kennedy, the assassinated president's younger brother, chief law enforcement officer, and Mafia fighter who regularly broke our criminal laws.

6. Director of the FBI J. Edgar Hoover, who aided all in the telling of lies.

Looking back, it seems that every move I made in my life drew me closer to someday unlocking the secrets of Dallas. In my legal career, I was a homicide investigator and jury trial prosecutor, the chief deputy attorney general of Delaware, and a murder defense attorney. Along the way I taught interrogation to police and wrote articles and a book about interrogation, *The Right to Remain Silent* (SMP, 1988).

In retirement, by the time I chose to tackle the secret mysteries of Dallas, I had handled over fifty-six homicide cases during the crime wave of the 1970s and 1980s. "Dallas" was to become for me the only intentionally unsolved homicide I had ever seen.

In taking on the challenges of this book, I knew what I was up against, and I knew that nearly everyone I was trying to reach would have a preconceived theory or opinion based on thousands of sources.

And now, with your permission…

CHAPTER TWO

The Elevator Conspiracy

With lightning speed, within the first week of the murders, Chief Justice Earl Warren was given the role of solving the three homicides and all the other crimes of that weekend. Tall and imposing, Earl Warren had agreed to head up a so-called "blue ribbon" investigative panel that we all know as the Warren Commission, but that virtually no one views today as "blue ribbon." Warren took the assignment at the urging of both Attorney General Robert F. Kennedy and President Lyndon Johnson. Were these men being "careful" in appointing Warren? Were they looking over their shoulders and seeing "international complications"? I wondered why Earl Warren, with his long-standing bias against law enforcement, would be given this role to solve the crime of the century.

In his role as chief justice, Warren was already infamous for having created the State Court Exclusionary Rule, the centerpiece of his personal criminal law revolution. Its harsh effects of suppressing police work are portrayed in the detective novel I wrote in 1988, which was based on homicides I solved, *The Right to Remain Silent*. That book, still in print while Warren's exclusionary rule flourishes in America, demonstrated the harm I perceived to have been inflicted on murder investigations by Warren's creation of a State Court Exclusionary Rule—one I opposed in Brooklyn Law School and spent my entire legal career contending with.

This handcuffing of state law enforcement in America began in 1961 when Earl Warren and his court met to discuss the case of *Mapp v. Ohio* and whether it should become against the law for a state government's voters to ban pornography. Earl Warren left that meeting with Justice William Brennan and held another more intimate meeting on another subject in a Supreme Court elevator. In that elevator it was decided they would ignore the Ohio pornography issues and turn the case into one that created a state court exclusionary rule that tossed out crucial evidence in a criminal case if a judge, usually intellectual and sheltered, determined that the evidence was seized by police using "unreasonable" methods.

In the process of establishing this rule, Earl Warren was aided by friendly justices, including Justice William O. Douglas, who soon would be revealed to be on the Mafia payroll in Las Vegas. Douglas was publicly exposed to be receiving an annual stipend of ten thousand dollars, all of which was derived from the proceeds of the sale of the Mafia's Flamingo Hotel and Casino, whose construction and related murder case is depicted in the film *Bugsy*.

Having Justice William O. Douglas on board gave the chief justice the votes he needed to take over the whole field of American criminal law and procedure by the power to suppress indispensable evidence, a power exercised by Earl Warren every day of the Warren Commission proceedings.

After Warren and Brennan stepped off the elevator, there were three bewildered justices about to learn that the *Mapp* pornography case had suddenly been hijacked. The justices not in on the elevator conspiracy became a dissenting minority.

Dissenter Justice Harlan labeled the surprise decision a "power grab." Harlan reprimanded Earl Warren for using "only a voice of power, not of reason," asking that the case be reargued.

Harlan's suggestion of a do-over was met with silence. The imperious cold shoulder is a tactic the chief justice used throughout the Warren Commission's ten-month triple homicide investigation.

Warren's cold-shoulder behavior explains why virtually no reader will be familiar with the names of the two star Dallas eyewitnesses, whose testimony was suppressed. Had each of their testimonies not been hidden by Warren, it easily would have proven there was a Mafia conspiracy in Dallas that killed three people and wounded another.

One of the two eyewitnesses was Mrs. Earlene Roberts, the housekeeper for Oswald's rooming house. Her testimony implicated two Dallas policemen in Oswald's attempted escape.

The other eyewitness was Dallas reporter Victor Robertson, a close-up eyewitness to Jack Ruby's first failed attempt on Lee Harvey Oswald's life to silence him by use of a gun at the Dallas Police Detective Division.

During the investigation, Warren was described by a staff member as "brusque." We will see evidence of this, and learn why, throughout our own investigation.

When I decided to try to solve all aspects of the Dallas case and take on the Warren Commission, I came prepared from years of studying Warren's ways, such as his vigorous support for the infamous internment of Japanese Americans during World War II and his extortion of General Dwight Eisenhower during his 1952 road to the White House. For the nomination, "Ike" needed California delegates that were controlled by Governor Warren. Ike offered Warren a Supreme Court justice seat for the delegates. In the classic model of extortion, Warren insisted on the chief justice job, and Ike caved.

Now in full charge of the Warren Commission, with maximum power as chairman and chief justice, Warren engaged daily in a blatant suppression of critical evidence like that provided by the testimony of Mrs. Earlene Roberts and Vic Robertson. Both witnesses were voluntary and sworn, and both ended up disregarded and muted in Warren's report.

In this book this professional homicide investigator and prosecutor shall return to these indispensable witnesses, their voices, and their highly trustworthy testimony.

CHAPTER THREE

Opening Statement to the Jury

This book will endeavor to unlock every single secret of Assassination Weekend in Dallas, with not a single mystery left unsolved. Every wrong answer from Earl Warren will be made right, restoring the truth and protecting that truth.

As well, it provides the heretofore unknown solution for the failure of the Bay of Pigs Invasion of April 17, 1961. I submit that you will find it is not merely what many other authors and historians assume: namely, that President Kennedy, a World War II hero in the Pacific, lacked the courage and decisiveness to provide air cover to the anti-Castro small brigade attack force of 150 Cuban exiles at the Bay of Pigs on the southern coast of Cuba.

Furthermore, this book will prove that failed invasion's causative connection, two years later, to the deadly events of the murderous weekend in November 1963. If not for the Bay of Pigs Invasion of 1961, President John F. Kennedy very likely never would have been assassinated by the Mafia in 1963.

Suppressing the Truth in Dallas provides the full answer for Lee Harvey Oswald's execution-style murder of Officer J. D. Tippit on the streets of Oak Cliff in Texas. The full answer, I submit, is not what other authors and historians assume.

Suppressing the Truth in Dallas provides the details of a cover-up never before uncovered, that is, how was Jack Ruby able to murder Lee Harvey Oswald, and why did he do it?

Chairman Warren falsely claimed in his final Warren Commission report on September 21, 1964, ten months after the assassination, that there was, in his words, "no evidence" of a conspiracy of any kind to assassinate President Kennedy and that there was "no evidence" that Jack Ruby was part of a conspiracy of any kind to silence Lee Harvey Oswald. Who was Warren protecting when he made that unsupportable finding that there were no other co-conspirators?

This book's legal analysis will demonstrate to your satisfaction that these two conclusions of "no evidence" of conspiracy were intended to deceive the voters.

Over the years, I have found myself at speaking engagements having to answer detailed questions that caused me to think more deeply about the "no evidence" conclusions. Ultimately, I felt that if I studied that which I taught young police to call EFW—every f'ing word—of the 888-page Warren Commission report and certain reputable sources identified in this book, such as the House Select Committee on Assassinations report of 1979, as a homicide professional I could follow the trail and unravel and expose Warren's conclusion that there was "no evidence" of a conspiracy of any kind as a deliberate cover-up. My experience told me that I could go well beyond merely proving there was *some* evidence of a conspiracy. I could do my best to prove the details of all the evidence of all the conspiracies and mysteries of Dallas. A tall order, perhaps, but homicide was my life's work.

It was my plan in this book not to rehash the ample "Dallas" and "JFK" evidence found in my bestselling book, *I Heard You Paint Houses.*

By tackling the job of researching and writing this book, it was my intention to create a rich and professional layer to the solutions of Dallas. A prosecutor must not only prove his own case; he also must disprove the criminal defense case. This I promise to do to your satisfaction in your role as the jury.

Before I started to read every assassination book I could get my hands on, I was persuaded by the fact that Earl Warren was a former professional law enforcement officer who had handled homicide cases. He was a former California assistant district attorney, district attorney of Alameda County, and attorney general before becoming governor of California. As a true professional in the field of homicide, with vast experience, more extensive than my own, Earl Warren could not simply have been making foolish mistake after foolish mistake in the basic conduct of his investigation.

The deeper I dug, the more the evidence revealed that Attorney General Earl Warren of the Japanese American internment camps, Governor Earl Warren of the extortion of Dwight D. Eisenhower, and Chief Justice Earl Warren of the formation of the exclusionary rule to suppress evidence knew precisely what he was doing in Dallas. I submit that it truly was Earl Warren himself who in his report was intentionally not solving the crime.

Along with the "how" and the "why," the whodunit will be revealed. Who did Earl Warren set out to protect with his cover-up? Names will be more than simply named; every fact will be analyzed as if presented to a jury.

I will draw on tips I learned from organized crime figures and FBI agents about how the Mafia operates and thinks in interviews for my three other nonfiction histories of the Mafia:

I Heard You Paint Houses (Steerforth Press, 2004), the biography of Hoffa assassin Frank "The Irishman" Sheeran, played by Robert De Niro in the movie adaptation, *The Irishman*. It was based on five years of tape-recorded confessions to me, echoing the long-ago advice I was given by the late Charlie Burke, an old-time Wilmington police detective, and his superior, Stan Friedman: *"They want to tell you, Choll."*

I co-authored *Donnie Brasco: Unfinished Business* (Running Press, 2008) with FBI deep cover agent Joseph D. Pistone, who bravely risked his life to infiltrate the Bonanno crime family for six years and whose countless days of testimony brought the Mafia to its knees—and put a half-million-dollar bounty on Donnie Brasco's head.

In *We're Going to Win This Thing* (Berkeley 2009), which I co-authored with Supervisory Special Agent Lin DeVecchio, whose Mafia Commission case destroyed the ruling commission, and therefore the Mafia itself, the Mafia sought revenge against DeVecchio by unsuccessfully framing him for murder.

I hope I'm not boasting when I make the point here that no author with a fraction of my life's experiences has analyzed the three homicides discussed in this book, the Bay of Pigs Invasion, or Earl Warren's cover-up of the crimes in Dallas.

Perhaps the most meaningful contribution of this book is its analysis of why the Mafia felt confident, and with very good reason bordering on certainty, that like James Bond, it had a license to kill. Quite literally, the Mafia could kill the president and get away with it.

By and large, "Dallas" authors are eager, fair-minded amateurs for whom this is their first and only homicide investigation.

Although I got a late start and the trail is cold, this is finally an effort to lay bare the truth by a professional with more than a little bit of background in homicide investigation, in the art of interrogation, and knowledge of the American Mafia.

Herein, you will find a cross-examination of the Warren Commission report. It is an interrogation of Chairman Earl Warren. It is a comprehensive investigation by a man who, as my mother's Italian family—the Di Marcos of Le Marche and Staten Island—would suggest, didn't "just get off the boat from the other side." At seventy-nine, I'm past my prime as a trial lawyer, but I wasn't born yesterday, and I'll do my best.

CHAPTER FOUR

Jesus, Mary, and Joseph

For my family, every minute of that weekend was a wretchedly sad forty-eight hours, tear-filled and physically draining.

"Why do they keep parading this Oswald?" I asked my mother and sister as Oswald went down yet another hallway with flashbulbs popping, television cameras focusing, and reporters shouting.

Three years before this madness in the hallways of the Dallas Police Department in 1963, a subdued top-secret meeting had taken place at the Kennedy compound in Palm Beach, Florida. That meeting would directly lead to the weekend of murder for Kennedy, Tippit, and Oswald.

President-elect John F. Kennedy was visited at the Palm Beach estate by the two highest-ranking members of the Central Intelligence Agency—Director Allen Dulles, a Princeton graduate, and Assistant Director Richard Bissell, a Yale economist and the next in line after Dulles's retirement.

Dulles and Bissell were in Palm Beach to brief the Democratic Party's president-elect on certain deadly top-secret CIA projects planned under the outgoing Republican president Dwight D. Eisenhower. Chief among these projects was the April 17, 1961, Bay of

Pigs Invasion, especially its planning in public places, and it would go on to play a significant role in the assassination of our beloved president and in Chairman Warren's cover-up. Trial lawyers refer to this category of proof as *causation*. "But for" certain events, would other events have followed "like the night, the day?"

At my mother's house we had no idea on that Sunday if the murderous weekend was over.

My mother was about halfway up the stairs to the bathroom when I said to her in disgust, "Oh, Jesus, they're parading him again. This is crazy. Somebody's going to shoot him. Oh…Jesus, somebody just shot him!"

In an instant my mother, Carolina, and my younger sister, Barbara, were at my side.

"Jesus, Mary, and Joseph. What next?" our mother said. "Is he dead?"

At that moment, Jack Ruby, the central figure of the greatest murder mystery in world history, was introduced to the world with a .38 in his hand under a pile of Dallas police officers.

Ruby fired that fatal shot that we all saw on television, and Lee Harvey Oswald was not Jack Ruby's only victim. What did this killing of Oswald by Ruby portend?

Thanks to Oswald we already had a president we hadn't chosen.

The pain in the house was tinged with bewilderment when, over coffee, we considered that the president's accused assassin, Lee Harvey Oswald, was a communist who had lived in Russia.

Over more bewilderment and more coffee, we considered Dallas police officer J. D. Tippit's murder by the communist Lee Harvey Oswald while Oswald was on the run. Then on Sunday, in the comfort of our homes, many of us would be eyewitnesses to Jack Ruby's murder of Oswald in cold blood during a carefully planned transfer of Oswald to another jail.

Was war coming? Nuclear war?

In the midst of worrying about our dead president's family, we listened to make sure that enough media time was devoted to the mysterious murder of Dallas police officer J. D. Tippit, shot on a suburban street in the Oak Cliff section of Dallas by Oswald forty-five minutes after Oswald had assassinated the president and forty-five minutes before his arrest that very Friday in a movie theater he had snuck into, where he had tried to shoot one of the brave arresting officers. Thankfully he was foiled in this last attempt.

We couldn't have guessed that while we were trying to digest it all, the late president's brother, Robert F. Kennedy, had far more important priorities than his brother's death.

Attorney General Robert F. Kennedy was absorbed in high-level damage control, the way President Johnson had been engaged on the recorded telephone call with Senator Everett Dirksen. This damage control is what Robert F. Kennedy and Lyndon Johnson had recruited Earl Warren for—"international complications" about which they had to be "careful."

What we didn't know was that the cover-up was already underway as we sat down to our dinners.

The next day, while our hearts were breaking at the sight of the late president's brother on foot in the funeral parade, now in the role of father to his brother's two toddlers, John-John and Caroline, no news reporters told us that Robert had interrupted his family duties to pay a visit to Earl Warren in his chambers in order to solicit the chief justice to stop whatever he was doing and to chair the presidential commission that was being formed by President Johnson. This commission was about to be given exclusive jurisdiction over the investigation and over crimes that Earl Warren would later admit in his 1977 memoir the federal government had absolutely no jurisdiction. All of these murders were committed under the exclusive jurisdiction of the Dallas police, including the assassination of a president, not a federal crime at that time.

CHAPTER FIVE

Ye Shall Know the Truth

In the newspapers, we were reassured that the government of Soviet Russia was taken by surprise by the assassination. The Russians were reportedly as confused as we were about the homicides. But who really knew?

Of course, we anticipated that answers were on the way, and never doubted they would be truthful answers. My family believed the Mounties always got their man and crime didn't pay.

Among the rags on the newsstand in those days was the Kremlin-controlled *Daily Worker*, a newspaper published for American Communists. Lee Harvey Oswald had promptly subscribed right after returning to America from Russia in June 1962, seventeen months before he was arrested for murdering both President Kennedy and Officer J. D. Tippit on the same day with weapons from the same source.

Meanwhile, what devilment was going on in Dallas? We stayed tuned. It was a free-for-all down there. What would be Attorney General Robert Kennedy's swift response? My family called the response we anticipated "kicking ass and taking names."

However, instead of action and truthful answers from our chief law enforcement officer, Robert F. Kennedy, and the Department of Justice, we became gradually and increasingly numbed by the absence of answers to a muddled mystery.

The Protestant King James Version of the Bible tells the world at John 8:32, "And ye shall know the truth, and the truth shall make you free." Ironically, this Biblical quote of wisdom is featured in the lobby of CIA Headquarters in Washington, DC, an organization whose planning and execution of the Bay of Pigs Invasion two years prior on April 17, 1963, it will be proven, helped to directly cause and cover up Assassination Weekend. Were it not for the CIA's role in the Bay of Pigs planning and invasion, Attorney General Robert F. Kennedy, the greatest crimefighter in American history, would have continued in his courageous and already largely successful three-year campaign to destroy the entire American Mafia, crime family by crime family.

During his post-arrest interrogation, Jack Ruby said about Chairman Earl Warren, *"Maybe certain people don't want to know the truth that may come out of me."*

Earl Warren simply ignored Jack Ruby's comment and left it on the table that uncovering the truth was not in Warren's interest, much less his quest. More importantly, Ruby's allegation against Warren should have been used by Warren as an entry point to get closer to the truth in his interrogation. "Jack, what part of the truth do you see me evading or avoiding?"

Meanwhile, we awaited word in neighborhoods like Flushing, demanding answers. What possibly could have blocked the truth from being revealed to us at once? Surely Robert F. Kennedy had access to every file and document and a legion of investigators in every law enforcement agency everywhere.

The secrets in need of suppressing by Warren revolve around the then–death penalty crime of felony murder, as committed by high-ranking government figures.

Simply put, in felony murder, a person commits a felony, such as armed robbery, and another dies in the stick-up.

16

My last jury trial in Delaware in 1976, prosecuting the death of a beloved schoolteacher, was to put four robbers on death row.

What were President Johnson's "international complications?" It doesn't take a PhD in psychology to know that *all* murder is something that one needs to be "careful" about.

CHAPTER SIX

The American Muddle

As news trickled in from Dallas, we observers found ourselves increasingly drinking muddied water.

There were many eyewitnesses to Jack Ruby's brazen gut-shot murder of Lee Harvey Oswald. I couldn't have been the only one to wonder about Oswald's safety in the face of jam-packed cameras, teeming microphones, and crowds of news reporters shouting questions. Oswald repeatedly declared he was just a "patsy," sneering his spurious claim of innocence, equating his not having been charged yet with his not being guilty. That is, until someone with extensive Dallas Police Department connections finally shot Oswald and locked his mysterious secrets shut inside him.

Could members of the Dallas police have done all the parading for the purpose of getting Oswald shot and suppressing his testimony?

We voters barely had time to digest the horror of President Kennedy's assassination when we were told by our media that Oswald had shot and killed a Dallas police officer named J. D. Tippit during Oswald's attempted flight on foot on a street in the Dallas suburb of Oak Cliff.

To a homicide detective gathering evidence, the act of flight from a crime scene is evidence of guilt. Running away is an admission of guilt as powerful as a signed confession.

Less than forty-eight hours after the president's assassination, Officer Tippit's murder, and Oswald's arrest, a portly Jack Ruby lunged forward and shot Oswald dead on Sunday morning, November 25, 1963, at 11:21 in the basement of the Dallas PD.

Did this murder inside the police department basement have anything to do with the murder of Officer Tippit on the street?

After killing Tippit, for reasons unknown, Oswald ducked into a movie theater to hide. Hiding, like flight, is likewise a confession.

Could all of this running and gunning by Oswald have been part of some elaborate escape plan? And in this line of work, "plan" is spelled CONSPIRACY.

That should have been homicide investigator Earl Warren's first thought and his first job to determine. The investigator in search of truth should not ignore the topic of "escape" as Warren did in his report.

Over the ensuing months we were shown still photos and were told that twenty-four-year-old Lee Harvey Oswald, before becoming a communist, was a United States Marine. Our collective jaws dropped. We knew what communism was, and it was perplexing that anyone, much less a Marine, would choose it.

While Lee Harvey Oswald was heading to Russia in 1959 to defect, the world was full of enslaved people who were trying to head the other way. These were people risking their lives from a border guard's bullet and often dying in order to escape from communist nations, which on penalty of death they were forbidden from leaving.

In the early 1970s when I was a homicide investigator and prosecutor in Wilmington, our office had the case of a beautiful young model who bought some take-out Chinese food for lunch to take back to her office and ended up cut to pieces, her body parts stored in the suitcase of one Cheng Wo Wa, an illegal Chinese employee of the restaurant. He was a merchant seaman who had jumped ship. In

1972 Earl Warren's Supreme Court ordered that self-governing voters could no longer have the death penalty statutes we had voted for many decades earlier. That meant that Cheng Wo Wa would escape execution for the horrible slaughter of this poor, innocent young woman. As a consequence, my superiors and the Wilmington police detectives decided to quickly deport him and turn him over to the Communist Chinese, who promptly executed him for the capital crime of jumping ship and leaving China.

Newspaper articles told us that in 1959, the year I started college, Lee Harvey Oswald, after his discharge from the Marines, had flown to Russia, defected, and tried to renounce his American citizenship and become a Russian citizen. We read that he slashed his wrists, attempting suicide because Russia had refused him citizenship. In response, Russia allowed him to stay as a legal alien. The media reported that Oswald lived and worked in a Russian factory for nearly three years and that he had married a pretty Russian woman named Marina before returning with her to America in June 1962, where, due to his surly behavior at work, they were to have relentless money problems. The couple reportedly had two infant daughters, one born in Russia and one born in America, adding to Oswald's money problems. The American baby was born a month before Oswald killed the president.

We were not told why Oswald returned to America, nor why he was allowed back in by President Kennedy's State Department under Dean Rusk after Oswald had attempted to renounce his citizenship.

The Oswald family, on arriving in America in June 1962, first settled and lived in the Dallas-Fort Worth area for some months before moving to New Orleans, where Oswald had spent a chunk of his early life and had relatives. One of these was his uncle, Charles "Dutz" Murret, an intimate of Mafia gangsters. Uncle Dutz, a former prize fighter and promoter, would provide funds to help Oswald get settled in New Orleans. One day, Oswald was arrested for disturbing the peace when, as a vocal supporter of Fidel Castro, he had a street fight with anti-Castro Cuban exiles while he was handing out pro-Castro communist literature.

Two months before Oswald killed President Kennedy and Officer Tippit, traveling alone, Oswald had taken a bus to Mexico City. There, using their real names, he applied for visas for himself, his pregnant wife, and his infant daughter to enable his family to return with him to Russia from Mexico City by way of Cuba.

Cuba deferred to Russia. Russia said it would take three weeks, but Oswald's visitor pass in Mexico only allowed him a few more days. Disappointed and angry, he vowed out loud that he would "kill that son-of-a bitch Kennedy." This threat was picked up on tape, as the CIA secretly bugged these offices. But it was not followed up by the CIA, so as not to reveal the taping.

The Oswald family next moved to the Dallas area. Prior to Jack Ruby's murder of Oswald, during the "parading" through the hallways, Dallas police charged Oswald with blowing off the top of President Kennedy's head from on high and from behind with a high-powered rifle on a bright, sunny day.

In photos we saw the glamorous thirty-two-year-old First Lady dressed in pink and spattered with blood sitting beside the president in their limousine called the Queen Mary.

Oswald also had been charged with wounding then-Texas Governor John Connally when, as it was later discovered by Warren Commission staffer Arlen Specter, a single bullet, derisively called the "magic bullet" (the second bullet of three fired from Oswald's sniper's nest formed by cartons of books) passed through the president and zigzagged into the governor, who was in the seat in front of the president shouting, "They're going to kill us all!" The governor survived his injury.

Coincidentally, staffer Arlen Specter was to become the prosecutor in the Teamster murder of Robert "Lonnie" DeGeorge, a rap that Frank Sheeran beat.

Although there have been some doubting amateurs, to a homicide investigator, the evidence is overwhelming that Lee Harvey Oswald fired the shots that killed President Kennedy and wounded Governor Connally.

Oswald worked in the Texas School Book Depository building. An announcement was made that employees would be allowed outside to watch the president's motorcade; thus Oswald knew he'd have the sixth floor to himself to build his small sniper nest.

Oswald was seen on the sixth floor of the building earlier that day. That floor was undergoing renovations that discouraged foot traffic.

A rifle Oswald had purchased by mail order was left behind on the sixth floor after the shooting. It was found fifty-two minutes after the president's assassination. To add to his evidence of guilt, Oswald got caught in a lie, later claiming he had never owned a rifle. Lying, like flight and hiding, is a form of confession.

Forensics proved Oswald's rifle had fired the shots. Witnesses on the floor below heard the firing of three shots above them and heard the shells hit the plywood floor. Three spent bullet casings were found on that floor. That morning Oswald had smuggled the high-powered rifle with its scope into the building in a homemade paper case. Oswald told his coworker, who drove him to work that morning, that he had curtain rods in the paper case.

The paper case was an easy fit over the rifle when the rifle was disassembled by the ex-Marine. Interrogators generally enjoy being lied to during interrogations. It leads to more evidence.

Oswald's escape by bus and taxi included lying to the taxi driver about where he lived, getting dropped off a few blocks past Earlene Roberts' rooming house, and walking back to it.

Again, flight is powerful evidence of guilt, as is fibbing to the taxi driver, as was fibbing about needing curtain rods. Confessions all. More confessions were to come, and all such evidence of guilt would be covered up and ignored by Chairman Warren and his investigators.

That Oswald killed President Kennedy with help in a conspiracy will be proven despite Earl Warren's suppression of massive evidence. The existence of each criminal conspiracy of Assassination Weekend will be exposed as another no-brainer when we sift through the Warren Commission report's own evidence. Despite Chairman Warren's efforts to conceal and protect Oswald's helpers, Oswald had them.

No one knew why Oswald killed again. But forty-five minutes after the president was assassinated, Oswald used his own recently purchased .38-caliber revolver to ambush Dallas police officer and World War II paratrooper J. D. Tippit during Oswald's attempted escape on foot through his Oak Cliff neighborhood.

That Oswald shot and killed Officer J. D. Tippit is another no-brainer for a homicide investigator. There were several eyewitnesses who identified Oswald as Tippit's shooter. One eyewitness picked up Officer Tippit's police radio and called in the shooting. Typical for that era, a few brave eyewitnesses followed Oswald to a movie theater and watched him sneak in. Eyewitnesses told the responding officers where in the theater they could find the killer of the murdered Officer Tippit. The police entered the movie theater. Oswald tried to shoot one of them with his .38 revolver, but in the struggle over the weapon the gun didn't fire, sparing the courageous officer, M. N. McDonald. That attempted murder of a policeman added still more powerful evidence of guilt in the assassination of the president.

The .38 in Oswald's possession in the movie theater was bought by him via mail order. Forensics proved that the .38 in Oswald's possession had been used to kill Officer Tippit.

That Oswald was the triggerman twice that Friday in Dallas was not a burning issue. My family and I remained convinced that the only issue in the case was why, and on whose behalf, Jack Ruby killed Lee Harvey Oswald. The single shot Ruby fired into Oswald's abdomen smacked loudly of conspiracy. We believed that Dallas police would make the connection between Oswald and Jack Ruby, and that was the key to everything.

We later read in the papers that Oswald's escape route on foot would get him closer to Jack Ruby's Oak Cliff neighborhood apartment. Magazines showed us an aerial view of that route. It looked to be less than a mile between Oswald's rooming house and Jack Ruby's apartment. This reeked of an Oswald and Ruby conspiracy, though was not yet proof beyond a reasonable doubt. The proof will come that links Ruby and Oswald in a conspiracy.

Oswald and Marina were not living together at the time. A month earlier, Oswald had rented a room in Oak Cliff under the assumed name of O. H. Lee. His use of an alias was more powerful evidence of guilt.

Juries don't like assumed names.

Oswald the Red recently had begun working at the Texas School Book Depository warehouse located right smack on the downtown Dallas route of the president's motorcade.

The route would pass directly below Lee Harvey Oswald's sixth-floor window. Magazines later traced Oswald's route from that window in the book warehouse to his Oak Cliff rooming house. Oswald entered the rooming house through the front door, making a pit stop at his room before proceeding toward the suburban neighborhood street where he would fatally shoot Officer Tippit.

Interrogation of his wife, Marina, unearthed a photograph of Oswald that Marina had taken at Oswald's request. It was a full-body portrait of Lee Harvey Oswald dressed in black, posing in a backyard with his mail-order .38 revolver in its holster at his waist and his mail-order Italian high-powered rifle raised in one hand. Oswald, in common with John and Robert Kennedy, was a rabid fan of Ian Fleming's James Bond 007 books. This photo portrayed Oswald as a man of action, like his hero 007, a man with a license to kill. Clutched in his left hand were two Marxist newspapers to which he subscribed: the *Militant* and the *Daily Worker*. He held them so that their front-page mastheads were prominently displayed. He posed as if advertising himself as an assassin for hire for Marxist causes. As if soliciting a contract to kill, Oswald sent a copy of the photo to *The Militant* with the words "Ready for anything."

That Oswald needed money is an understatement. Marina was pregnant with their second child, and he couldn't hold down a job.

Oswald's mother, Marguerite Oswald, with her husband having died young and leaving her with two boys to raise, was obsessed with the need for money while Oswald was growing up. It permeated the atmosphere.

Oswald's wife took his mother's place in that department. George de Mohrenschildt, a Russian émigré, and his wife befriended the Oswalds and tried to help the young couple. George testified before the Warren Commission about Marina Oswald: *"She was annoying him all the time. 'Why don't you make some money?'"*

Advertising with his guns "ready for anything" would be a way to get Marina "some money." That issue of the *Militant* that Oswald held in the photograph had an article that called retired right-wing general Edwin Walker a fascist. Soon after the photo was taken, Oswald attempted to assassinate General Walker.

After her son's televised murder by Jack Ruby, Marguerite Oswald saw lost dollar signs in book deals, lost revenue she blamed on competition from the Warren Commission report's sales. Marguerite said, *"Money-wise I got took."* She added that the Warren Commission *"took the bread and butter out of my mouth."*

No wonder her son resented capitalism.

In 1979, just over fifteen years after President Kennedy's death, voters were told something unusual in the annals of homicide investigation. The House Select Committee on Assassinations was created to re-examine the work of the unsatisfactory Warren Commission investigation. We learned that the Dallas Police, the FBI, and the Warren Commission, but ultimately Earl Warren, had overlooked an eyewitness to Officer Tippit's murder.

Jack Ray Tatum had significant new evidence to offer that was consistent with J. D. Tippit's autopsy.

This testimony first confirmed what was already known from other eyewitnesses, namely that Officer Tippit was seen talking to Oswald through the passenger window of Tippit's squad car. Officer Tippit then exited the driver's side of his police car and did not remove his service revolver from his holster nor order Oswald to raise his hands over his head. Tatum said that once out of his police car, Tippit began to walk toward the front of his police car, empty-handed, when Oswald whipped out his .38 from his jacket and opened fire across the hood of the police car, striking Officer Tippit in the chest.

Jack Ray Tatum then added information that, once confirmed, constituted evidence that Lee Harvey Oswald was a member of a CONSPIRACY, something Earl Warren wanted desperately to suppress. Earl Warren's motive shall be revealed.

After shooting Officer Tippit, Oswald walked away to the rear along the police car's passenger side and past the trunk of the police car, essentially leaving the scene.

Oswald changed his mind, did a military about-face, and walked back to Officer Tippit's car, continuing back along the driver's side of the police car. When he reached Officer Tippit on the ground near the front wheel, Oswald mercilessly shot Officer Tippit point-blank in the temple, executing the police officer and obviously silencing Tippit forever.

The public had not been told about that silencing of Tippit because that was evidence from an eyewitness that, I submit, Earl Warren had managed not to find. There would be more intentionally undiscovered but highly important witnesses.

Meanwhile, in 1963 we learned that President Kennedy was not Lee Harvey Oswald's first political shooting in Dallas. That spring, seven months before Assassination Weekend, on April 10, 1963, after 9:00 p.m., and acting alone, Oswald fired through the window of the Dallas home of right-wing anti-Castro activist and retired general Edwin Walker, aiming at Walker's head while he sat at a desk doing his taxes. A month prior to this attempt on his life, Walker, forcibly retired for distributing right-wing literature to his subordinates, had publicly called for the United States military to "liquidate" Oswald's idol Fidel Castro. This threatening speech by Walker was reported in the March 5, 1963, issue of Oswald's hometown newspaper, the *Dallas Times Herald*.

Pro-Castro communist Oswald immediately put General Walker under surveillance at Walker's home, taking photographs of the scene. Within a week after the general's speech threatening the liquidation of Castro, Oswald bought his mail-order high-powered Mannlicher-Carcano Italian rifle with a scope. Oswald was "ready for anything."

Oswald's plans included hiding his rifle in some bushes in the alley behind Walker's house until he could return to the scene to get the murder weapon with the help of Marina, now his co-conspirator. Lee Harvey Oswald had plotted his getaway from Walker's house to his own home. It would be by public bus, just as he would later board a bus following his assassination of President Kennedy.

However, firing from behind a tree across the alley, Oswald missed the general's head with his single shot when the bullet nicked the windowpane. Oswald escaped from the scene by bus without a trace.

Although my family and I had watched Jack Ruby kill Oswald on Sunday November 24, 1963, it would be fifty years before I endeavored to push through the muddle and try my hand at unlocking the secrets of Dallas.

No doubt I was influenced by certain things Frank Sheeran had said to me during our five years together while I interrogated him for what became Frank's biography, my book about Jimmy Hoffa's murder, *I Heard You Paint Houses.*

In our first interview I inadvertently referred to Lee Harvey Oswald as a "lone cowboy." Panicked, Frank blurted, *"I'm not going anywhere near Dallas."*

We didn't speak again for eight years.

When we did, he revealed that some days to weeks before the shooting in Dallas, without knowing why, he had delivered a bag of three or four high-powered rifles to Maryland on orders of Mafia capo Tony "Pro" Provenzano. A decade later Frank was told the rifles had been used to assassinate the president. However, Frank had no idea how they would have been used or why there were multiple rifles. Frank guessed there might have been alternate motorcade routes.

CHAPTER SEVEN

No Evidence

In my law enforcement career I was conscious of the experiences of two extremely bright men, writers William F. Buckley, Jr., of Yale and Norman Mailer of Harvard. Their intelligence in so many fields led each to enter the field of homicide investigation and to champion the cause of a convicted murderer. Each had read the transcripts of his particular murderer and resolved that the police and courts were incorrect and these men were innocent. Each resulted in the release of his man, as I would later cause the release of a convicted murderer. Upon release Buckley's man, a rapist and murderer, attempted to kidnap and kill a Greek woman by stabbing her in a car. With a knife sticking out from her ribs, she furiously fought him off and survived.

Mailer's man, Jack Henry Abbott, murdered a prison guard and subsequently authored the prison memoir *In the Belly of the Beast*, which Mailer helped him promote. Shortly after Mailer aided his release, Abbott fatally stabbed a waiter who was an aspiring playwright and who had told his killer that the delicatessen's bathroom was not open to the public.

As a result of these separate cases I developed a distaste for amateurs investigating any crimes, much less homicides.

Over the years, as I looked at new assassination book covers, I discovered that few of the countless writers of assassination books had any homicide experience. The most prominent was Warren loyalist and Manson family prosecutor Vincent Bugliosi. But he had been a prosecutor, not an investigator. While there is overlap, there is a distinction between prosecuting and investigating homicides in both experience and skill set. Overwhelmingly, armchair detectives with no law enforcement experience of any kind had written the "Dallas" books of the day, as they largely had written the Hoffa books.

The dictionary-sized September 21, 1964, Warren Commission report was released to the world following a ten-month investigation by what President Johnson repeatedly described as a "blue ribbon panel." It consisted of seven commissioners, including its chairman, Earl Warren.

The new president had created the panel before a week, including Thanksgiving, had passed following his predecessor's assassination. By Black Friday, the commission was in place. Obviously, President Johnson and Robert F. Kennedy viewed "international complications" with great alarm to mandate such great haste.

Five of the seven commissioners were selected by President Johnson. The two whom Johnson had not personally selected had strong ties to the CIA. Both had been selected secretly behind the scenes by Attorney General Robert F. Kennedy.

After waiting ten months for the Warren Commission report, instead of getting a rush of truth, on September 21, 1964, we got controversy that exists to this day.

In his report, Warren wrote: *"The Commission has found no evidence that either Lee Harvey Oswald or Jack Ruby was part of any conspiracy, domestic or foreign, to assassinate President Kennedy."*

No evidence? No evidence at all?

On the face of it, a suspect being serially, and at the time legally, interrogated had permanently been silenced in the Dallas Police Department basement by Jack Ruby, a man with Mafia and Dallas PD ties. That alone is evidence that an interrogation was interrupted on purpose in a Dallas police station, in a room packed with police officers, by an infiltrator with a gun. These facts are not "no evidence" of a conspiracy. These are all leads to be followed, but they weren't.

In his report, Chairman Warren decided that strip club owner Jack Ruby had acted impulsively and completely by himself, that is, without any help from a co-conspirator, in killing Oswald. Ruby did this after penetrating the heavily guarded Dallas Police Department basement. Warren claimed that Ruby committed this murder from a deep and uncontrollable wellspring of grief that turned him into a one-man vigilante, setting out to prove that "Jews are tough" and from a desire to spare Jacqueline Kennedy the ordeal of returning to Dallas to testify at Oswald's murder trial.

I wondered, was this the same Jack Ruby I watched deliberately step out of the police parade, in a crouch, get close enough for his .38 revolver to be effective, and purposefully and accurately gut-shoot Lee Harvey Oswald, who was handcuffed to a Dallas detective? There was nothing impulsive about Ruby's skillful, cold-blooded movements, mostly staying low until springing out from his crouch.

And that part about the clip joint owner with a heart of gold who sacrifices his own life, liberty, and pursuit of happiness to spare the First Lady's feelings as he imagined them to be? Who on Earth wrote those lines? Did Chief Justice Earl Warren think we voters were born yesterday?

In our neighborhoods, we knew hoodlums like Jack Ruby personally, and we knew that the only time a hoodlum would care about a grieving widow was when he was trying to squeeze a buck out of one.

From the beginnings of my career as a homicide investigator, which began in early 1971, less than seven years after the release of the Warren report, the misgivings I had about the report's publicized conclusions became magnified by the reality of my new career solving homicides. By then Earl Warren was into the tenth year of his criminal law revolution, and by giving the truth a back seat to artificial case-killing rules that were dictated to us at a fast pace, homicide investigations were hampered and still are.

Fifty years later when I decided to do my homework, I read the Warren Commission report and analyzed Earl Warren's unethical promotion of an obvious pack of lies by Jack Ruby. I developed some sympathy for the much-maligned so-called conspiracy theorists. Instinctively, these writers knew there had been a conspiracy and a cover-up by someone, but many got lost in the facts and counterfacts.

CHAPTER EIGHT

Voters in the Dark

Days after the brutal events in Dallas, it sunk in that the arrested assassin Lee Harvey Oswald, shot dead by Jack Ruby, had stolen my enthusiastic first vote from me. Oswald had disenfranchised me in an era where voting rights were deservedly always front and center, especially as in 1963 the right to vote was being denied to Black voters in the South. Laws at the time mandated the paying of poll taxes that poor Black voters couldn't afford and the passage of literacy tests to qualify to register that couldn't be passed by poorly educated Southern Blacks. If the literacy tests were mandated in New York City, they couldn't be passed by my Italian grandparents, who were illiterate in two languages. When my grandmother Rosa said, "Kiss the ground in America," she said it in the Italian dialect of Le Marche.

Poof went our right to vote for our president, that most important and vital of all our rights, the basis for the right to govern ourselves, the single thing that made us no longer peasants.

For us common neighborhood folk, questions would pop up over a cup of coffee, but there were no answers. Who had the motive to kill President Kennedy and replace him with Vice President Johnson?

Was it a segregationist from the South, the kind that had killed Black civil rights leader Medgar Evers with a high-powered rifle the day after President Kennedy's infamous civil rights speech? To whom did such a change of command matter? What policy of the Kennedy administration would be stopped if the president was dead?

History now sees that President Johnson relied on the Dallas tragedy and the memory of the martyred president as a means to plow through and continue President Kennedy's civil rights work with the passage of the 1964 Public Accommodations Act and the 1965 Voting Rights Act, federal laws that ultimately and for all time abolished legal segregation, making racial discrimination illegal and abolishing impediments to the full right to vote. Five days after the assassination President Johnson invoked President Kennedy's memory and in his honor addressed Congress: *"We have talked long enough in this country about equal rights.... It is time now to write the next chapter and to write it in the books of law."*

In his speech, Johnson was establishing links of causation that ultimately would lead to our first Black president.

Voters had no way of imagining that martyred President Kennedy, with his father's help, had added a wrinkle to our right to vote and to govern ourselves during the 1960 election cycle by allowing the Mafia to pour money into the Kennedy campaign in West Virginia and Illinois.

This fact was established to the satisfaction of G. Robert Blakey, chief counsel to the 1976–1979 House Select Committee on Assassinations. According to Blakey, Mafia money had funded the "High Hopes" campaign of candidate John F. Kennedy in the West Virginia primary, provided by Chicago godfather Sam Giancana through Frank Sinatra.

We had no way of imagining that, during his 1960 meeting with CIA officials Allen Dulles and Richard Bissell at the Kennedy compound in Palm Beach, and ever since he came to power until the day of his death, President Kennedy had been breaking our duly enacted criminal laws.

We certainly had no idea, nor could we possibly imagine and would not believe if we were shown proof, that President Kennedy had made a secret illegal conspiracy deal with the Mafia, one that broke the country's criminal laws and that was not to be fully exposed by the Senate until 1975.

CHAPTER NINE

More Catholic than the Pope

Chief Justice Earl Warren and his followers had already demonstrated in case after case that he was the right man to suppress evidence the commission might uncover, especially involving the Mafia or Cuba, which you will see are the topics with the greatest fear factor among government officials in Washington, DC; Alexandria, Virginia; and Gettysburg, Pennsylvania.

Following Chairman Warren's appointment to head the "blue ribbon" panel of the Warren Commission by President Johnson, Warren took to work with him his methodology and his shrewd skills at taking over all things, even on an elevator.

Midway through his investigation, on June 7, 1964, Earl Warren presided over the interrogation of Jack Ruby in Dallas. Commissioner Gerald Ford asked Jack Ruby about trips he had made to Cuba. Chairman Warren began interrupting and talking about something else. One of Jack Ruby's lawyers, Joe Tonahill, described it: *"Ford never did finish his interrogation on Cuba. Warren blocked Ford out on it. That was very impressive, I thought. Ford gave him a hard look, too. I was sitting right there and saw it happen."*

Thomas Mann, President Johnson's ambassador to Mexico at the time of the Warren Commission's work, reported that within a few days after his brother's death, Robert F. Kennedy, whose supervisory jurisdiction did not include the CIA, had nevertheless ordered the CIA not to investigate any possible Cuba connections to the assassination. Ambassador Mann told the *Chicago Sun-Times* newspaper: *"If the president's brother thought Oswald did it entirely on his own, I don't see why I should be more Catholic than the Pope."*

To a homicide investigator, the fact that both Earl Warren and Robert F. Kennedy suppressed investigative talk about Cuba means, at a minimum, that Cuba had some kind of role in the assassination of President Kennedy.

During the investigation and in his report, Commissioner Warren suppressed the mighty role of Cuba. As well, Earl Warren suppressed the truth of a Mafia conspiracy being the force behind the Kennedy assassination, as clearly it was. Chairman Warren was to demonstrate a suppression of the truth such as he had evidenced in his creation of the exclusionary rule, where lofty definitions from his own constantly changing dictionary were all that mattered. The truth came in last and got suppressed in a new court proceeding judges began to call a suppression hearing. Chairman Earl Warren suppressed the truth in Dallas as if he were conducting one of his newly created suppression hearings instead of a triple homicide investigation.

CHAPTER TEN

The Rubber Stamp

By Black Friday, the day after Thanksgiving 1963, exactly one week after the midday assassination of President Kennedy, the late-afternoon execution of Officer Tippit, and five days after the midmorning murder of Lee Harvey Oswald, President Johnson, our president for one week, had already appointed his "blue ribbon" commission of seven members, and each had accepted. On that Friday, November 29, 1963, it was announced that the commission was tasked to investigate the three homicides in Dallas and to report truthfully to the American voting public.

Voters had no idea that this panel was, in actuality, the driving force of a rubber-stamp scheme to tamper with the three homicide "investigations" and fix them according to a script.

Earl Warren's appointment as chairman, it was claimed in the press, would give the commission colossal prestige and stature, as if a homicide investigation needs either.

"Hey," said the homicide detective, "please pass the prestige and stature."

In the final paragraph of the announcement, the White House Press Release of November 29, 1963, stated: *"The president is*

37

instructing the Special Commission to satisfy itself that the truth is known as far as it can be discovered, and to report its findings and conclusions to him, to the American people, and to the world."

So as of that day we would know the truth. Now you're talking, Mr. President! But excuse my curiosity, what's all that secret talk about "international complications?"

The first practical effect of this announcement of a blue ribbon panel was to guarantee that there would be no other official oversight investigation, such as a normal congressional investigation by the House or Senate Judiciary Committees.

President Johnson's hand-picked commission would provide the final word to the triple homicide. It would be the only official conclusion. The FBI, the Secret Service, and Dallas PD might have their thoughts, but their conclusions would be subordinate. President Johnson had cornered the market. This blue-ribbon panel creation was what Johnson meant in his warning to Senator Dirksen of their needing to be *careful.*

President Johnson personally contacted segregationist senator James Eastland of Mississippi to block him from conducting a Senate investigation, which he otherwise would have done. Chairman of the powerful Senate Judiciary Committee, Eastland had already asserted his committee's jurisdiction over the investigation of the assassination by proposing to introduce legislation to make it an FBI-investigated federal offense to kill a president. This Eastland bill was merely an excuse for a Judiciary Committee investigation with Eastland at the helm.

At that time the only murders the FBI had jurisdiction over were those committed in a national park, on an Indian reservation, or occurring during a kidnapping or bank robbery. Accordingly, the special agents of the FBI almost never had the opportunity to get homicide experience. The FBI had no homicide squad and no homicide investigators.

Senator James Eastland of Mississippi was a "Dixiecrat," a staunch segregationist Democrat, and proud signer of the Southern

Manifesto that swore to uphold segregation. Senator Eastland was a consummate politician who was in the midst of defying the Kennedy brothers' intention to give Blacks the right to vote in the South and the Kennedys' intention to use the power of the federal government to enforce Earl Warren's *Brown v. Board of Education* decision and President Eisenhower's two Civil Rights Acts of 1957 and 1960. Senator Eastland was planning to filibuster and defeat President Kennedy's proposed 1963 Civil Rights Act. At least that had been the plan prior to the assassination.

Senator James Eastland of then-blatantly racist Mississippi was a long-standing member of the Senate with a great deal of seniority and many favors owed to him by other senators over the years. At the time of the assassination, Senator Eastland might have been the last person in politics in Washington whom President Johnson could count on to help cover up even slight wrongdoing by the Kennedy brothers.

I had occasion to hear about Senator Eastland's power over presidents during a chat with then-Senator Joseph Biden in a Wanamaker's Department Store in Wilmington, Delaware, in 1976. Newly elected president Jimmy Carter had announced during his campaign that when he won he would take away from the senior senator of each state, and give to each state's Democratic party chairman, the selection of United States attorneys, federal prosecutors, and the selection of United States Marshals, political plums all. Based on my record in law enforcement, Delaware's Democratic state party chairman Henry Topel had asked me to be the United States Attorney of Delaware, but Carter took back his pledge. In our chat, Biden imagined that Senator Eastland had called Jimmy Carter to give him the facts of life. Biden arched his back and did an imitation of Eastland in Biden's best Southern drawl: *"Jimmy, I really do trust you want to get along with the Senate. Now Jimmy, let's understand each other. Nobody is going to pick a United States Attorney or a United States Marshal in the State of Mississippi but me."*

A "Dixiecrat" politician like Eastland would have relished the opportunity to expose felonious wrongdoing and lawbreaking by President Kennedy in the course of a Senate investigation into his murder.

Director J. Edgar Hoover and his FBI had attempted to assert its federal jurisdiction of the assassination on the tenuous grounds that a bullet nicked the windshield of the president's Lincoln limousine, thereby and by sleight of hand conveniently turning the case of the assassination of the president of the United States into the case of vandalizing government-owned property, a federal crime.

It will be proven that it was Director Hoover's intent to speedily prepare an FBI report with the hidden goal of excluding any possibility of exposing a conspiracy of any kind, which, by following the yellow brick road, could easily lead to the exposure of a Mafia conspiracy, which in turn could put a shame on President Kennedy's legacy and could expose some notable living Washington figures, including Hoover himself, to felony murder charges.

This book's consideration of the impact of the felony murder rule on Warren's cover-up, to the best of my knowledge, appears nowhere prior to the above sentence, not even in the report of Earl Warren, a former district attorney who prosecuted felony murder cases.

As discussed earlier, felony murder is the rule of law that allows prosecutors to charge a participant in the commission of certain felonies with the crime of first-degree murder should even an unplanned death occur in connection with the commission of the felony. The person so charged need not have been at the scene of the felony. It's sufficient for the charge that the person participated in the conspiracy or planning to commit the felony, like robbery. The person so charged need not have known that one of his accomplices even had a gun. It would seem impossible for a former prosecutor with Earl Warren's experience to not know that felony murder is what he needed to suppress most of all.

It will be proven that once Hoover's report was received, and with felony murder at stake, Earl Warren's panel would be expected to rubber-stamp Hoover's FBI report and nip felony murder in the bud before anyone like Senator Eastland could stir up the pot.

In *The Memoirs of Earl Warren* (Doubleday and Company, Inc., 1977) the chief justice wrote about the triple homicide: *"The federal government, with the FBI, the Secret Service, the CIA and other agencies, had no clear jurisdiction of the subject. They were in the investigation merely by sufferance of the local and state authorities of Texas, because at that time it was not a federal offense to assassinate a president, or to murder the assassin as Ruby had done. Either was a state crime, as were other cases of murder."*

All those participating in the cover-up knew that.

If President Johnson wanted to make sure to keep the assassination investigation in the hands of Director Hoover and out of the hands of others in Congress, the president and the director had to work fast, and against certain members of Congress.

Senator Everett Dirksen of Illinois was the ranking Republican on Senator Eastland's Judiciary Committee. Before our naval hero president's body was buried in Arlington, Senator Dirksen announced that public hearings would begin promptly after the Thanksgiving weekend. Senator Dirksen said, *"No time will be lost."*

Hearing those words that were a threat to him, no time was lost by President Johnson. At once, using the White House telephone with its secret tape-recording system, Johnson called this man with whom he had worked in the Senate for many years for the purpose of herding Senator Dirksen onto the prairie.

These recorded conversations and the other White House telephone tape recordings referred to herein are recounted in chronological order with useful commentary in author and Warren Commission report supporter Max Holland's *The Kennedy Assassination Tapes* (Knopf, 2004).

President Johnson said on tape as much as he needed to say to Senator Dirksen to rein him in: *"[W]e got some international complications that could come up to us if we are not careful."*

For the public, grief was still the only issue, not "international complications" that required us to be "careful."

What does President Johnson mean in plain English? Clearly, by his choice of words, he was getting Senator Dirksen to back off. He was getting the senator to ultimately forego what was a golden opportunity for historic and publicity-drenched Senate hearings, with Dirksen in the number two chair. But this was a president calling, telling Dirksen there were "international complications," without spelling them out. A year prior the world had almost come to nuclear war over the "international complication" known as the Cuban Missile Crisis.

And why shouldn't Eastland, Dirksen, and their committee handle this duty, as was their right, and do so in public hearings so the voters of the day would not have their heads spin and, in the spirit of self-government, could learn what was going on in their White House?

To the public, these would be indecipherable words: "*international complications.*" Dirksen didn't want to know any more. All he wanted to do was hang up. Dirksen didn't ask the president a single question. What international complications? How "careful?" Dirksen didn't feel a need to point out that these three homicides were domestic crimes, not international crimes.

Shortly after this warning to Dirksen, and of grave concern to those powerful men who had committed felony murder and who prayed for a speedy cover-up, there came an announcement that in his public hearings the powerful, bigoted Senator Eastland planned on using the services of Communist-hunting Jay Sourwine as his chief investigator. Sourwine, on behalf of Eastland, would sink his teeth into the Kennedy brothers' legacy with relish, thereby jeopardizing Johnson's run for the presidency in 1964.

To prevent these threatening things—a tough Sourwine investigation, "some international complications" that would "come up to us" from an open Senate Judiciary Committee investigation—President Johnson smoothly talked Senator Eastland out of holding Senate hearings.

To win over Senator Eastland, and even though it would make a larger Warren Commission that would be harder to control, President

Johnson increased the number of commissioners from his original plan of three to seven. The original plan was to have the chief justice and two hand-picked civilian commissioners with CIA backgrounds do the rubber-stamping of a Hoover FBI report finding "no evidence" of a conspiracy and no sign of the Mafia or Cuba.

Knowing he needed to soothe Eastland and his Senate Judiciary Committee, and that next he would need to soothe the House Judiciary Committee, President Johnson told Senator Eastland that there would be seven commissioners. The additional four would consist of two senators and two representatives, one from each party. That's how you investigate a homicide, isn't it—get two investigators from each party? But as the evidence will prove, the commissioners and the legal staff were not to be engaged in a homicide investigation, merely the *appearance* of one.

On White House recordings the very day after the assassination, President Johnson expressed to Senator George Smathers, a Florida Democrat, one of the things that was driving this rubber-stamp cover-up in Johnson's view: *"President [Kennedy] is a national hero... and we've got to keep this Kennedy aura around us through this [1964] election."*

With John F. Kennedy's "aura" at stake, President Johnson successfully repeated in the House of Representatives the same tactics he had used on the Senate Judiciary Committee.

Speaker of the House John McCormack, a Democrat from Massachusetts, is heard on White House recordings replying to President Johnson: *"Well, as far as the House is concerned, I'll stop...I'll do anything that I can to stop investigations."*

FBI Director Hoover was already all in. He told President Johnson in a White House telephone conversation that he would have his Bureau do an FBI report proving that there was no conspiracy to kill the president.

The scheme between Director Hoover and President Johnson was that, once formed, the seven-man commission would merely review the FBI report that was about to be done and approve the FBI's conclusion that Lee Harvey Oswald was both a lone wolf assassin and a lone wolf police killer, and that Jack Ruby was a lone wolf killer of a lone wolf assassin.

In beautiful plain English this was a cover-up proposal by the FBI director of twenty-eight years. What Hoover and Johnson were saying actually meant that the fix was going to be in on all this murder and that the Warren report was, from its inception, a rubber stamp of an FBI report. Less than a week after the assassination, the FBI's report was ready to be distributed, yet no one raised an eyebrow at the speed of its creation.

As President Johnson is heard saying repeatedly as he signed up all his Magnificent Seven Commissioners by that Friday, *"All you're gonna do is evaluate a Hoover report that he's already made."*

President Johnson was recorded telling Georgia Democrat Senator Richard Russell, in recruiting him to the commission, that there would be *"...about a seven-man board to evaluate Hoover's report.... He's ready with it now and he wants to get it off as quick as he can."*

Johnson told Russell on tape: *"All you're going to do is evaluate a Hoover report that he's already made.... But you're goddamn sure gonna serve."*

Not a single person on the other end of Johnson's telephone ever asked him why Hoover needed no time at all to investigate and prepare a report on three extremely complicated homicides, each with its own trail that could lead many places. Two killings were done by a pro-Castro Communist and another by a strip club owner thug with Mafia connections, Cuba connections, and Dallas Police Department connections who, with a gun in his pocket, infiltrated the security of the Dallas PD basement and arrived at the exact time and location of his target in that basement.

The specifics regarding Ruby's connections to various members of the Dallas PD alone would take weeks of investigation. Ruby's connections to the Mafia underworld would take weeks more. Ruby's phone records showed telephone calls to Mafia types increasing in number as the date of the assassination neared.

Weeks could be spent on a list of those with motives to kill President Kennedy and checking out their alibis.

While Attorney General Robert F. Kennedy's fearless feud with the Mafia and Jimmy Hoffa was public knowledge, a squad needed to spend some time investigating its relationship, if any, to the killing of the president.

After his conviction, Mafia capo Tony Provenzano held an obscene press conference in Miami, which ensured that the media would know just how much he hated the attorney general and the president.

Fidel Castro had made a threat in an American newspaper against President Kennedy. Investigating that threat alone was a full-time job.

Weeks could be spent on the April 17, 1961, Bay of Pigs Invasion and on the 1962 Cuban Missile Crisis.

Johnson calling Hoover's report "ready" can only mean that his report is part of a conspiracy to cover up.

Meanwhile, each man President Johnson said those words to about evaluating a report that Hoover was going to prepare for their seal of approval had IQs high enough to go to excellent colleges and really good law schools. Yet each had absolutely no reaction to Johnson's assertion that Hoover was "ready" to solve these homicides for them.

The commission would have to give the appearance of investigating, like a boxer taking a dive, and Warren had to be at the ready to suppress the witnesses, like Earlene Roberts and Victor Robertson.

Meanwhile, later that same day, as he recruited commissioners, President Johnson is recorded explaining to Republican Representative Charles Halleck of Indiana: *"It's got some foreign complications, CIA and other things."*

Johnson added to Representative Halleck that the job description of a Warren Commission commissioner called for *"...somebody that's had some experience with these CIA matters...."*

Halleck wasn't the slightest bit curious.

There were profound things that needed suppressing, and Earl Warren was the right man for the job.

On December 17, 1966, three years after the assassination, President Johnson and his personal lawyer and future disgraced and dismissed Supreme Court justice Abe Fortas were recorded reminiscing about their efforts to keep Texas official Waggoner Carr from starting his own investigation in November 1963. Fortas said about that earlier time:

"You were desperately working with (sic), and I was helping you to prevent a Texas investigation."

"That is correct," said Johnson.

"Well," said Fortas, "we went through the tortures of the damned to prevent the damn thing. And we finally got [Waggoner] Carr up here and had the chief justice go to work on him, too."

CHAPTER ELEVEN

Permanent Ink

Former President Eisenhower, and the rest of those caught up in "international complications," had to know they were in excellent hands. They had to trust that Earl Warren would handle this felony murder scrape just as he had handled other tough political issues, such as any fallout from his drive to uproot Japanese American families without a hearing and send them to internment camps during World War II. With his political tools, he undid the damage that internment had caused him.

As California's attorney general, Earl Warren was all for internment and testified that Americans had been "lulled into a false sense of security" by the peaceful Japanese Americans.

After Warren won that debate and internment was funded, Fred Korematsu, a Japanese American who refused to leave his home for an internment camp, brought a court challenge case, eventually making its way to the United States Supreme Court. While the war was still going on, and in a six-to-three decision, Attorney General Warren was pleased to read that the internment policy had been upheld. On the accusation of racism, the court held that racism was not involved in the policy, but then Earl Warren turned the page and read the scathing dissent.

Although they have no legal effect of any kind, all dissents are always printed along with the majority opinion. They are carved in stone as part of the decision itself. They go wherever the decision goes, as would Justice John Marshall Harlan's attack on the "power grab" by Warren in *Mapp v. Ohio* in 1961.

Within this dissent in *Korematsu* were the seeds of a several-decades-long public debate in which the issue was framed as one of racist motivation on the part of those like Warren who aided and abetted the government's mission of "exclusion"—excluding Japanese Americans from living in certain strategic areas on and near the Pacific Ocean, that is, living in their homes.

Associate Justice of the United States Supreme Court Frank Murphy dissented from the majority opinion in the bitterest possible language. Justice Murphy took deadly aim and fired volleys at those leaders like Earl Warren, who had helped implement the imprisonment of 110, 000 Japanese Americans.

To Justice Murphy this was neither a legal issue nor military strategy about which reasonable minds might differ. To Justice Murphy the written opinion of the six justices in the majority fell "into the ugly abyss of racism."

Murphy compared those who thought and acted like Warren to Italian fascists and German Nazis. He labeled what Warren and others had done as equivalent to the "abhorrent and despicable treatment of minority groups by the dictatorial tyrannies which this nation is now pledged to destroy."

Justice Murphy wrote that the government's "racism" was "utterly revolting." He added, *"I dissent, therefore, from this legalization of racism."*

In the vitriolic chosen language of his dissent on December 18, 1944, Justice Murphy would keep the debate grounded in racism over the years and long past Earl Warren's death in 1974. Having been publicly humiliated to such a degree by Justice Murphy, and having been so damaged by the charge of racism, Warren never even tried to defend himself or the voters who supported internment. He could have asked Justice Murphy "what race?" Young American men were being killed and maimed defending the Chinese, Manchurians, and Koreans.

In the years before the 1941 sneak attack on Pearl Harbor, American moviegoers and book readers loved the brilliant haiku-writing Japanese detective character, Mr. Kentaro Moto. A devout Buddhist and judo master portrayed in eight films by Peter Lorre, Mr. Moto was a box-office rival to the Charlie Chan detective movies of that era. In the Kaufman and Hart comedic play, *The Man Who Came to Dinner*, there's a line in homage to the Japanese American detective: *"Think fast, Mr. Moto, think fast."*

Yet Earl Warren took his lumps and remained silent, a tactic often recommended by publicists to keep their clients, such as politicians, from stirring the pot and giving legs to bad publicity.

Chief Justice of the Supreme Court Earl Warren would die having once been branded a racist by a Supreme Court dissent written in permanent ink.

Following Murphy's dissent, Warren spent thirty years trying to live down the accusation. In his decisions he sought to prove that he was actually a champion of civil liberties. After all, he created the criminal law revolution. By the time of his appointment as a blue-ribbon chairman, he was universally idolized.

I was in a minority opposing his criminal law revolution in opinion articles, a detective novel, and speaking engagements.

CHAPTER TWELVE

He Knew He Was Chairman

If enough turns of the handle were made on the jack-in-the-box, dangerous truths would pop up all over the place.

Chairman Warren would keep the lid on the box with help from the two professionals who understood "the CIA picture" and by dominating the congressmen and the legal staff.

Future United States senator Arlen Specter was hired as a member of the fourteen-lawyer legal staff, the young worker-bee lawyers under the supervision and control of Chairman Warren. In his memoir *Passion for Truth* (William Morrow, 2000), Specter recalls Chairman Warren's intimidating and domineering treatment of the commission staff investigators. Arlen Specter wrote in his memoir: *"Earl Warren was justly revered for many of his skills and qualities, but his treatment of his staff was not one of them...."*

Did Earl Warren rely on his legal staff? Specter wrote about those ten months that he worked for the commission: *"The initial staff meeting with Chief Justice Warren was the only such session ever held... we were never again called for a general session."*

That's the best way to keep a lid on three murders. A detective captain who did that would be sent down to patrol, at best.

Hypocritically, at that one and only staff meeting, Chairman Warren began by stating: *"We have only one client, the truth."*

Since everyone in the room was a lawyer, they were all bound by the canons of ethics to adhere to the truth at all times and in all cases. Telling a lie is punishable by disbarment, at the least, as was to happen to our two disbarred presidents Nixon and Clinton, who each won a lifetime achievement in the Pinocchio awards.

Arlen Specter learned from then–Republican congressman of Michigan and Warren Commissioner Gerald Ford, later President Ford, that the six subordinate commissioners fared no better with Chairman Warren than had the fourteen legal staff members like Specter. Ford told Specter:

> *He knew he was chairman. In fact, he made a number of decisions that, at least in the original few months, were unilateral. And that upset some of the commission members, who thought he had delegated to himself too much control and authority.... There grew up some tension between the commission members and the chairman because of some of the actions we thought should have been reviewed by and acted on by the commission as a whole.*

The "original few" hours, much less months, are more often than not the heart and soul of any homicide investigation. That's when it all happens. The chairman made "unilateral" decisions during those "original few months" that had to have been important decisions. They had to have been important enough to cause "upset" to commission members.

Was this merely a clumsy style of management, or did Chairman Warren, like Director J. Edgar Hoover and President Lyndon Johnson, with their rubber-stamp strategy, have a planned outcome in his mind that he intended to reach, for which he needed to keep both the fourteen-member legal staff and the other six commissioners in line and under what Arlen Specter called his "brusque" authority?

How else could he manage to pull off a cover-up of the assassination conspiracy between the Mafia, Ruby, and Oswald but by "brusque" authority, taking full charge and making unilateral decisions?

"There was no deviation from his schedule and his scenario."

Trying out a truthful and plausible scenario is something homicide detectives do to arrive at the truth, something detectives regularly do. As Sherlock Holmes instructed Doctor Watson in Arthur Conan Doyle's "The Lauriston Garden Mystery": *"It is a capital mistake to theorize before you have all the evidence. It biases the judgment."*

As it turns out, what Chairman Warren's scenario was all along, from his first conversation with President Johnson, each without a shred of evidence in their briefcases, is the verdict the public got in the end. There was no deviation from his scenario. Warren simply kept his hand firmly pressed down on the lid of the jack-in-the-box, and anyone who tried to turn the handle would get smacked down, as did Gerald Ford when he tried to ask Jack Ruby questions about Ruby's connections to Cuba, a topic that easily could have led to felony-murder Bay of Pigs evidence coming out of Ruby's mouth.

CHAPTER THIRTEEN

The Creation of the Commission

There was to be no "scenario" of a conspiracy of any kind to be found anywhere in Dallas from the moment President Johnson signed on to the idea of the creation of a commission.

Once Johnson became committed to the idea of a presidential commission, the appointment of Earl Warren to chair it was made with the express approval of Attorney General Robert F. Kennedy, who had set aside his funeral duties and gone to Warren's chambers to explain to him the necessity for the commission and Warren's role in it.

Did Robert F. Kennedy take time away from his grieving family to secure Warren as chairman because he knew that a cover-up was needed to preserve his late brother's reputation, his legacy, his "aura"? The evidence will prove it to be one of two motives, the second being that Robert F. Kennedy himself needed the cover-up for what his civil rights enemies like Senator Eastland would consider the AG's own felony-murder crimes. These were crimes that his supporters would say were patriotic operations that he approved on behalf of his country during a time of cold war and betrayal by worldwide communist aggression.

The bloc of six subordinate members of the commission was designed by President Johnson and Attorney General Kennedy to have two civilian members on it.

John J. McCloy would be one of the two civilian members. The White House tapes reveal that McCloy was one of the two commissioners not actually selected by President Johnson, but selected behind the scenes by Attorney General Kennedy.

By virtue of experience, John J. McCloy was right for the job of purposefully *not* solving the three murders, and like Warren, by ignoring the Mafia, Cuba, Earlene Roberts, and Victor Robertson.

McCloy was the assistant secretary of war during World War II. As such, he had implemented the Japanese American internment policy and in that capacity had known Earl Warren for many years. After the war McCloy, then married to the daughter of a partner of financier J.P. Morgan, was appointed the first World Bank president.

Two years later McCloy became the military governor of postwar Germany. In that position he pardoned and released from prison several convicted Nazi war criminals. Chief among them was the convicted Nazi armament manufacturer Alfried Krupp. For crimes against humanity at the war trials, Krupp was sentenced to twelve years and had all his vast property confiscated.

From prison, Krupp had plotted to have his enormous wealth restored. He hired a New York lawyer, a friend of McCloy's, to spring him. This lawyer was willing to work on a percentage basis. McCloy, ignoring conflict-of-interest rules, released Krupp after he had served a mere three years of his twelve-year sentence. McCloy returned to Krupp all of his property and many millions of dollars. A split of that was a nice haul for McCloy's lawyer friend, who had to have been grateful that his friend McCloy had released Krupp from prison with his assets.

Nevertheless, as President Johnson would phrase it, did McCloy comprehend "the CIA picture"?

In 1947 when the idea of a Central Intelligence Agency was first suggested to President Harry Truman he was against it, calling it an

"American Gestapo." However, McCloy intervened on the side of the pro-CIA faction and became, in a very real sense, the founding father of the CIA.

What was this man who had championed the CIA and was long supportive of its role now doing on the Warren Commission? Obviously, in the end he was a man who could be counted on to see the importance of going along with the cover-up for the sake of important friends and the sake of the CIA that he had founded.

Nearly every historian on the subject writes that Robert F. Kennedy and Lyndon Johnson hated each other, and that the attorney general made sure that during his brother's presidency, Vice President Lyndon Johnson was kept in the dark as much as possible. Many called Robert F. Kennedy "the real vice president."

President Johnson described what his aides called the "Bobby problem": *"That upstart's come too far and too fast. He skipped the grades where you learn the rules of life. He never liked me, and that's nothing compared to what I think of him."*

Whatever Lyndon Johnson and Robert F. Kennedy were covering up for the sake of self-preservation—perhaps in Johnson's case preserving the "aura" of President Kennedy for the next election, or in Robert F. Kennedy's case to avoid indictment for felony murder—was sufficient grounds for them to work together as they did in the act of convincing Warren to lead their conspiracy and in appointing McCloy.

As noted, all six of the subordinate members of the Warren Commission were lawyers, as were their fourteen-member staff counsel, including Arlen Specter. Very lawyerly, properly, and professionally giving at least the appearance of an investigation, John J. McCloy sought to question Jacqueline Kennedy. As an eyewitness she would have been indispensable to any homicide investigation. She saw and heard all the action from her seat in the car next to President Kennedy. Do you want to know how many shots she heard? Ask her. Do you want to know from which direction they came? Ask her. Do you want to know if the president mentioned any mortal enemies he feared or any work he was engaged in that he thought might be personally dangerous? Ask her. Was there any pillow talk between them that would shed light on his assassination? Ask her to think long and hard.

As if Chairman Warren were trying to reinforce Jack Ruby's claim that his primary motive to kill Oswald was to spare the widow from testifying before a jury in Dallas, Chairman Warren ordered McCloy to spare the widow from testifying.

McCloy replied that they had to question her. He said: *"She's talking about [the assassination] at all the cocktail parties in Washington."*

Warren then allowed an abbreviated deposition to be taken, which he then brusquely and rudely cut off after nine minutes, the way he had cut off Gerald Ford's attempt to interrogate Jack Ruby about Cuba. Chairman Warren didn't care about appearances beyond those nine minutes.

Arlen Specter wrote of it: *"The interview omitted most of the lines of questioning I had proposed. It was almost worthless."*

This decision by Warren to commit prosecutorial malpractice by ignoring an eyewitness was one of many tactics he used to secure his lone-wolf scenario for his forthcoming report. Chairman Warren gave the same gag order regarding two other indispensable homicide eyewitnesses: President Johnson and his spouse, Lady Bird Johnson. All members were forbidden to ask a single question of these two occupants of a limo that was directly behind the Secret Service limo that was directly behind the president's limo. As a non-Ivy Leaguer whom Kennedy's people referred to as "Uncle Cornpone" behind his back, how fully could Johnson be trusted during questioning? Would his answers spill over onto the covering up of his own butt at the expense of his nemesis Robert F. Kennedy?

Attorney General Kennedy, while delivering to the Mafia on a silver platter bloody motive upon bloody motive to kill any Kennedy on sight many times over, would certainly be questioned extensively by even an incompetent homicide investigator. At a minimum, in charge of combating organized crime, AG Kennedy likely would be in a position from his own office's wiretaps and informants to know if there were any others like Tony Provenzano out there whose blood boiled, like Senator Eastland's, at any mention of the Kennedy brothers.

Robert F. Kennedy knew that as attorney general he had authorized many then-illegal bugs and wiretappings of Mafia bosses, but he hid this treasure trove from the Warren Commission and the public.

Earl Warren allowed the AG to place himself off limits to any questioning. Robert F. Kennedy would not be a witness in the investigation.

A rookie detective would not need his older partner to point out that these choices by Chairman Warren were not the product of mere incompetence. They were the product of subversion. Chairman Warren was looking out for the best interests of Attorney General Kennedy, among others.

Warren had relied on Kennedy to personally enforce the chief justice's civil rights rulings, and these two giants of the civil rights movement had a bond and well-earned mutual respect.

CHAPTER FOURTEEN

The Mafia's Motive

With his breathtakingly brave service on the Senate Rackets Committee, followed closely by his nearly three years as attorney general, Robert F. Kennedy was the most knowledgeable man in America about corrupt labor unions and the Mafia. In 1957, as chief counsel to the Senate Rackets Committee, he interrogated then Teamsters' president Dave Beck into a tailspin. *The Chicago Daily News* reporter covering the Beck Teamsters case wrote: *"The closing half hour on Wednesday was about the finest half hour I've ever seen on Capitol Hill."* This interrogation by Kennedy resulted in the uncovering of evidence that sent Beck to jail for, among other things, using union funds to build his son a house.

In a different Senate hearing, chief counsel Robert F. Kennedy had called Mafia Commission member and Chicago boss Sam Giancana "a little girl" for giggling.

In 1960 Kennedy wrote a book targeting corrupt labor unions, *The Enemy Within* (Harper, 1960). The *New York Times Book Review* stated: *"Mr. Kennedy exposed himself and his family to terrible danger for three years."*

He signed on for more danger for himself and his family when his brother appointed him attorney general in early 1961. As AG, Robert F. Kennedy formed his own private "Get Hoffa Squad," whose professional diligence gave Jimmy Hoffa, Dave Beck's replacement as Teamsters president, thirteen years of jail time for misusing union funds and jury tampering.

As mentioned, Attorney General Kennedy's Department of Justice had put Genovese capo and Teamsters vice-president Tony "Pro" Provenzano in jail for a seven-year stretch for extortion. His conviction for selling labor peace to trucking companies in New Jersey cost Provenzano millions. Attorney General Kennedy warned the prosecutor he had hand-picked to take Provenzano to trial, Matthew P. Boylan: *"They will try to kill you."*

Boylan was to get his man, but it was Kennedy that Tony Provenzano blamed for his conviction and jail sentence and, most importantly, for losing his lump sum pension.

Just before Robert F. Kennedy took over the attorney general's office in 1961 there were 35 organized crime convictions under the Eisenhower administration. In 1963, under Attorney General Kennedy, there were 288 organized crime convictions, and the number was swiftly rising. These were all headline cases.

The Mafia viewed the appointment of Robert F. Kennedy to the post as a deep betrayal. Mafia bosses in Chicago and New York believed they had helped John F. Kennedy become president in the first place in 1960 by delivering West Virginia's union vote in the Democratic primary, and in the general election by delivering big bucks and Illinois voters, whether living or dead, while Vice President Johnson delivered Texas.

In October 1963, about a month before Assassination Weekend, Mafia turncoat and Genovese crime family soldier Joseph Valachi of East Harlem was paraded before the television cameras for two weeks of interrogation by the Senate Rackets Committee. Attorney General Kennedy introduced Joe Valachi to the world for the sole purpose of exposing the Mafia's secrets to the light of day for the first time ever, including the ritual of associates becoming "made" members, and including Valachi's confession to thirty-three murders.

"*This here,*" Valachi testified, "*what I'm telling you, what I'm exposing to you and the press and everybody, this is my doom.*"

"*The only way the Mafia could operate for as long and as well as it had, was through airtight secrecy,*" said Supervisory Special Agent Lin DeVecchio of the Mafia Commission case. "*Attorney General Kennedy went after the Mafia with Joe Valachi's testimony where the Mafia was most vulnerable, in the daily newspaper.*"

At the close of Joe Valachi's testimony, Attorney General Kennedy said before the cameras of the world that the Valachi hearing was "*the greatest intelligence breakthrough in the history of organized crime in America.*"

Attorney General Robert F. Kennedy added: "*Because of Joseph Valachi we know that [the Mafia] is run by a commission…and that the leaders in most major cities are responsible to the commission…and we know who the active members of the commission are today.*"

Who could have imagined that in a month this "greatest intelligence breakthrough" would become worth less than Monopoly money?

The attorney general and the world had no idea there was a commission until the debriefing and Senate testimony of Joseph Valachi, whose father had sold fruit and vegetables in a street market to support his family.

But one thing is for certain, every associate, soldier, capo, consigliere, underboss, and boss who was a member of the Mafia's secret society blamed Robert Kennedy for using the despicable Valachi to make a name for himself among the voters at the expense of their secret society's racketeering livelihood. Over the years there had been the odd prosecution of a gangster, such as Lucky Luciano, but nothing like this Kennedy onslaught. Before Valachi, voters had no idea that all these gangsters were connected to each other and by a blood oath.

Voters learned from Joe Valachi that the commission was formed in 1931 at a meeting in Chicago called by New York City gangster boss Lucky Luciano and attended by the territorial bosses, including Al Capone of Chicago.

In 1948 Earl Warren had campaigned unsuccessfully as the Republican vice-presidential candidate. Warren's running mate was New York Governor Thomas Dewey. Dewey had successfully prosecuted Lucky Luciano using wiretaps, which were then legal under the voters' laws of New York. Luciano was convicted of using nice-looking young Italian men to ask out pretty Italian girls and eventually lead them to a location where they were gang-raped, drugged with heroin until addicted, and forced into prostitution.

From Valachi's riveting testimony we learned in October 1963, with mouths wide open, that the commission Luciano had created consisted of the five New York families and the Chicago and Buffalo families. It had seven male commissioners, just as Warren's commission was about to have a month later in November 1963. In the face of the headlines generated by Attorney General Kennedy, to the godfathers' way of thinking, they had no choice but to kill the president and put his brother out of the business of destroying their own private Cosa Nostra.

What did the secret racketeering world of the Mafia have at stake as they watched the October 1963 Valachi hearings?

From Manhattan on the Atlantic Coast to Manhattan Beach on the Pacific Coast, the billion-dollar Mafia empire flourished as a secret monopoly in pitch darkness at the time of President Kennedy's 1960 election and before Robert F. Kennedy was named attorney general. In such darkness, by keeping its world secret, as a nation within a nation, divided into geographic territories but working together and getting its own way, they controlled the Teamsters Union's billion-dollar pension fund as its private bank; the political structure of America's major cities; the ownership and building of Las Vegas; the American waterfront; big city police departments; bookmaking; the nation's major unions; the nation's most famous night clubs; truck hijacking; United States senators, congressmen, and governors; at least one United States Supreme Court associate justice (William O.

Douglas of the elevator conspiracy); and much more in legitimate and illegitimate businesses. Importantly, as it relates to this investigation, they also controlled Havana, Cuba, before Fidel Castro kicked out the Mafia in 1959 and took over all their casinos, racetracks, shrimp boats, sugarcane fields, and under the banner of communism, every single other vestige of capitalism.

While proof of motive is not mandatory in a criminal prosecution, prosecutors are permitted to prove motive to strengthen their cases. Under the word "motive" in the Mafia's dictionary is Robert F. Kennedy's picture.

In 1994 the Mafia and Jimmy Hoffa lawyer Frank Ragano wrote a memoir appropriately called *Mob Lawyer* (Scribner, 1994). In the memoir, Ragano claimed to have listened in on a discussion between Jimmy Hoffa, Chicago gangster and Teamsters official Joey Glimco, and Teamsters lawyer Bill Bufalino in early 1963 while Hoffa grand juries convened by Attorney General Kennedy were meeting in Nashville and Chicago. While playing gin with Glimco, Hoffa asked Bill Bufalino, *"What do you think would happen if something happened to Booby?"*

Reportedly, Hoffa always referred to his archenemy as *Booby.*

The consensus reached in the discussion was that if something happened to his kid brother, President Kennedy would unleash the dogs. But if something happened to President Kennedy, Vice President Johnson would become the president, and it was no secret that Lyndon hated Robert Kennedy. LBJ, it was agreed, definitely would get rid of Kennedy as attorney general. According to Frank Ragano's recollection, Jimmy Hoffa said, *"Damn right he would. He hates him as much as I do."*

Add to the list this most powerful motive possible: On April 4, 1961, when sixty-year-old Carlos Marcello, the New Orleans territorial boss whose Mafia territory included Dallas, showed up at the immigration office for his routine check-in as required by deportation proceedings brought by Attorney General Kennedy, the portly, five-foot-two-inch Marcello was stunned by being placed in handcuffs.

He was flown to Guatemala possessing only the money he had in his pocket and the suit and tie he wore in his capacity as a New Orleans businessman who owned a canned tomato company.

The young Robert F. Kennedy, attorney general for three months, justified his unprecedented dirty trick by claiming that in order to avoid deportation to Italy, Marcello had spread some money around in Guatemala and procured a false Guatemalan birth certificate.

From Guatemala, Marcello sent for his lawyers and family. He attempted to return to New Orleans, but the United States refused his visa request, while granting visas to his entourage.

Marcello was put in a truck with his American lawyer and driven deeper into Central America, where he was told to get out of the truck and walk eight miles through the jungle to an airport. Along the road he slipped into a ravine and broke three ribs, a painful injury, especially for a portly person on foot in a hot jungle.

To add insult to kidnapping, when Marcello finally managed to return to the States the New Orleans and Dallas boss was greeted by an $850,000 tax lien and a separate federal criminal indictment. As well as the tax lien, Attorney General Kennedy had charged Carlos Marcello with fraud against the government by attempting to use a fake Guatemalan birth certificate to sabotage his deportation.

One of AG Kennedy's main federal prosecutors, G. Robert Blakey, later to become chief counsel of the House Select Committee on Assassinations, prosecuted the federal trial in New Orleans. On the afternoon of November 22, 1963, three hours after President Kennedy had been assassinated, the jury, having heard news of the assassination from the trial judge, returned a prudent verdict of not guilty for Carlos Marcello.

Earl Warren's suppression of the nuts-and-bolts evidence of a Mafia conspiracy to assassinate President Kennedy was successful. Like Mrs. Earlene Roberts and reporter Victor Robinson, the Mafia was also ignored in Chairman Warren's report.

But why was the Mafia so protected by Warren?

Over the years there has been much suspicion of a Mafia conspiracy, including an expressed belief by G. Robert Blakey that the "mob killed Kennedy and got away with it." Notwithstanding the professor's hunch, this book contains the nuts-and-bolts detailed case against the Mafia with relevant and trustworthy evidence beyond a reasonable doubt, the standard of proof I lived by in my career presenting homicides to juries.

And like the old comic-book optical illusion where children are asked to find the vase in a drawing and the borders of the vase are the profiles of twin men, one profile on each side of the picture, once you see the vase you never fail to see it again.

In 1977 prosecutor Gary Cornwell became the deputy chief counsel to the House Select Committee on Assassinations, the number-two investigator behind G. Robert Blakey. Cornwell wrote in his book *Real Answers* (Paleface Press, 1998):

> *[O]ne of the major areas of investigation that we focused upon was a possible Mafia conspiracy, both because the Kennedy administration's crackdown on organized crime, headed by the president's brother, Attorney General Robert Kennedy, clearly gave the Mafia a motive that made them suspects in the case, and because it appeared that at least Jack Ruby, if not Oswald, had Mafia connections.*

Before Congress let the funding run out, Blakey's committee discovered a number of Mafia connections of Ruby in both Dallas and Cuba. According to British journalist John Wilson Hudson, who was confined in a Cuban jail in 1959, Ruby visited an inmate, Florida and Cuba's Mafia boss Santo Trafficante. Blakey's committee found evidence that Ruby got Trafficante out of Castro's jail.

Regarding transcripts of the FBI's illegal electronic surveillance, such as phone taps and room bugs in the early 1960s, Cornwell observed: *"Most of the major organized crime families, with two prominent exceptions, Carlos Marcello in New Orleans and Santo Trafficante in Florida, were the subject of this eavesdropping and the transcripts contained numerous conversations where killing Kennedy was proposed, discussed and debated by Mafia leaders."*

It's a shame Carlos Marcello and his close friend Santo Trafficante apparently had not been much included by AG Kennedy and his FBI in the early 1960s illegal tapping and bugging, especially after Marcello's return to New Orleans from Guatemala. His anger toward Robert F. Kennedy, like the anger of Tony Provenzano, would have fried up the wires.

Cornwell doesn't explain why Carlos Marcello was not the subject of an illegal bug the minute he landed home from his kidnapping journey. It was a perfect time to bug and tape an irate boss. Considering that Robert Kennedy never testified to the commission, the existence of any of the Mafia tapings never had to come up.

CHAPTER FIFTEEN

Stacking the Deck

The formation of the squad that would be called the Warren Commission, together with its membership list, was announced to the reporters covering the White House on November 29, 1963. From his farm in Gettysburg, former President Eisenhower was quite pleased with the commission and its membership.

Many journalists questioned the appointment of former CIA director Allen Dulles when they saw his name on the roster. Four days after one of the most emotional days of Americans' lives, President John F. Kennedy's televised funeral procession took place with a black riderless horse, boots pointed backwards in the stirrups, accompanied by a brave and beautiful grieving widow and two fatherless children the public had come to love as family.

The appointment of Allen Dulles to the commission raised a few eyebrows based on the grim events of the U-2 incident of early spring 1960. Six months before the November 8, 1960, election that gave John F. Kennedy the presidency, one of the last publicized duties that twice-elected President Dwight D. Eisenhower carried out in his last of eight years as president was to look into the eyes of the voters and tell a huge Pinocchio lie at a brinksmanship moment in the Cold War. With the hands-on help of his CIA Director Allen Dulles, Ike deliberately and repeatedly fed lies to the self-governing voters. Worse, that string of lies, however well-intentioned and in the interest of a greater good these two men believed their lying to be, Allen Dulles and Dwight Eisenhower humiliated American voters when quickly incontrovertible proof of their lying was broadcast out from the Kremlin to the world at large.

Ike and Allen Dulles's lying was done to cover up an incident occurring on May 1, 1960—May Day to the communists of the world. On that day, during the height of the Cold War, a Russian missile downed an American U-2 plane some 1,300 miles inside Russian sovereignty.

Believing the CIA plane to have been obliterated by the missile and the pilot killed, Ike's CIA advisers, led by the pipe-smoking, womanizing CIA director with the Clark Gable mustache, Allen Dulles, all came to the rescue like the king's horses and the king's men trying to put Humpty Dumpty back together again. They fell back on a cover-up story, which was a convincing lie, the nature of which would provide the CIA with what they called "plausible deniability."

In the first week of May 1960, following the shooting down of the encroaching U-2 plane, Ike cleared his throat, looked us in the eye on the television monitor, faked being angry, and assured voters that the U-2 plane was not a spy plane. He cleared his throat again and told us it was an innocent weather reconnaissance plane that had drifted off course because the pilot's oxygen supply had malfunctioned. With the pilot deprived of oxygen and either dead in the plane from asphyxiation or hopelessly passed out, the weather plane kept traveling on automatic pilot, trespassing deeply into forbidden Russian airspace, until the dastardly Russians fired a missile at it, killing the pilot.

We all believed Ike. His denial was more than plausible. Everyone liked Ike. At age twelve in 1954 in our basement in Flushing I painted an oil paint-by-numbers portrait of the great American hero, the mastermind of the D-Day invasion, and hung it on the wall. Ike had won his two elections in landslides. His administration was going to get to the bottom of the oxygen malfunction by the mandatory grounding and inspecting of all Lockheed U-2 aircraft and by repairing those U-2 planes that might malfunction in future weather flights.

The American public largely blamed Russia for being trigger-happy. We couldn't understand why the Russian government didn't contact our government before shooting down our poor pilot who might still have been alive in that plane before the missile hit it. The Russian Reds had a weatherman's blood on their hands.

With a historic Paris Summit conference coming up in two weeks to establish better relations leading to a lasting peaceful coexistence between the nuclear nations of the United States and Russia, Ike, the heroic former general rightly credited with leading our brave Allied troops to victory in Europe, huddled conspiratorially with Dulles and stuck to his guns. An innocent American pilot on a weather mission was the homicide victim of a Russian missile. Was the pilot a married man? Did he have children?

Six days later, on May 7, Russian dictator Nikita Khrushchev announced, *"I must tell you a secret. When I made my first report I deliberately did not say that the pilot was alive and well...and now just look how many silly things the Americans have said."*

So much of the Cold War seemed to be fought on the battleground of public relations—on the issue of how the Communists or Americans looked to the rest of the world. What any side did was often less important than how they looked doing it.

Per his training, the "alive and well" CIA pilot, Kentuckian Francis Gary Powers, already had confessed to being a spy. Photos of his largely undamaged plane were paraded before the cameras, and it was shown to be a spy plane with nothing on it that had anything to do with the weather.

Tellingly, Premier Khrushchev blamed it all not on Ike, our president, our elected leader, but on Allen Dulles, whom Ike had installed as CIA director when Ike took over the presidency in 1953. Khrushchev urged the people of the world to "seek a reply from Allen Dulles, at whose instructions the American aircraft flew over the Soviet Union." It was as if Allen Dulles, not Ike, was the official in charge in Washington.

Three and a half years later in November 1963, in that first week following what the brand-new president Lyndon Johnson on White House tape crudely called the "shootin' scrape" in Dallas, it was boldly revealed that one of the seven commissioners officially appointed by President Johnson (this one secretly appointed by Attorney General Kennedy) was the retired director of the CIA, Allen Dulles, a past proven intentional liar in the U-2 incident and many others. It was at that moment that every last one of the other commissioners, if they didn't know already, had to have gotten a flash of guilty knowledge that with Dulles on board, they were about to be engaged in an operation of plausible deniability disguised as a triple homicide investigation.

CHAPTER SIXTEEN

Loading the Dice

President Johnson was the first to follow his own advice to be "careful." He used his political skills to stack the seven-member jury of commissioners with CIA-friendly men, votes he could count on by men who understood "international complications." And so, four of the six subordinate commissioners below Warren had had direct, strong, well-known, and open ties to the CIA. During Johnson's telethon campaign for support in establishing the commission under Chief Justice Earl Warren, President Johnson expressed his "careful" strategy on a White House tape. To minority whip Representative Leslie Arends, Republican of Illinois, Johnson made it clear that all the commissioners being selected were required to comprehend "*...the CIA picture, you see....*" Arends, like the others, did not say, "Huh, how's that? What CIA picture?"

How did every one of these government officials like Arends know what the "CIA picture" was?

At the beginning of that week of selecting commissioners, Republican Senator Everett Dirksen received a serious warning from President Johnson on White House tape. As we know, Senator Dirksen didn't say, "Huh, how's that? What could 'some international complications' that could 'come up to us' and 'the CIA picture, you see' possibly have to do with the fanatical communist and Castro idolizer Lee Harvey Oswald, dead Dallas policeman J. D. Tippit, strip club owner Jack Ruby, and our revered President Kennedy?"

President Johnson selected Earl Warren, John J. McCloy, and Allen Dulles for the commission. He also personally selected the other four commissioners, the congressmen, but only after he ran their names by FBI Director J. Edgar Hoover on tape.

Practically against the senator's will, President Johnson selected Senator Richard Russell, a Democrat from Georgia, who'd been Lyndon Johnson's Senate mentor. These men from Georgia and Texas were two sons of the Confederacy. Russell was in charge of the Senate subcommittee that governed the CIA's funding, and, as such, he was a partisan supporter of the CIA and its activities.

The other senator was required to be a Republican, so Johnson selected the potentially pliable Senator John Sherman Cooper, renowned for working closely with Democrats. While President Johnson had to appoint a Republican senator, he selected one who relied on Kennedy Democrats to get elected and chose Cooper.

From the House of Representatives, President Johnson selected the Republican representative from Michigan and future president Gerald Ford. This was a twofer. First, Ford had a similar job in the House as Russell had in the Senate. Ford sat on the largely secretive House subcommittee in charge of CIA funding and, as such, was a partisan supporter of the CIA and the projects he funded. Second, Representative Ford made a secret side agreement with the FBI to keep Director J. Edgar Hoover and his FBI informed of all the confidential day-to-day goings-on of the Warren Commission as it met privately in sessions only open to the commissioners and their staff. As he later admitted, Representative Ford was Hoover's mole in the commission, which was supposed to be doing its work behind closed doors.

The deputy director of the FBI under Hoover years later wrote:

Hoover was delighted when Gerald Ford was named to the Warren Commission. The Director wrote in one of his internal memos that the Bureau could expect Ford to "look after FBI interests," and he did, keeping us fully advised of what was going on behind closed doors. He was our man, our informant on the Warren Commission.

In selecting Ford, President Johnson had told Representative Leslie Arends on secret tape that he was looking for "someone that's pretty familiar with the defense picture, the foreign relations picture, and also the CIA picture, you see, the Hoover picture."

Huh? What did the FBI and Hoover have to do with "the CIA picture, you see?" Hoover had no supervisory responsibility over the CIA. What did all these "pictures" have to do with three dead men, one wounded governor, and two scared-to-death wives in Dallas? Yet on tape they all seemed to know what Johnson was talking about without having to be told.

There is no way President or Lady Bird Johnson ever would be allowed to testify under oath. The new president, although left out of a lot of White House secret meetings by the president's brother, truly did have the whole "picture." He knew too much to be allowed to testify, or to want to.

For the final selection of the busy week of plotting while giving the appearance of mourning, President Johnson chose a loyal Democratic congressman from New Orleans, Louisiana, Hale Boggs, the representative of Carlos Marcello and his Mafia home base, the city of New Orleans.

Ten years earlier in 1953, a group of businessmen in New Orleans, worn down by the rampant and blatant corruption of the New Orleans Police Department, created the Metropolitan Crime Commission. Its first director was Aaron Kohn, who remained in office from 1954 to 1978. Kohn had retired from the FBI with a reputation as a fearless agent who had helped put desperadoes like John Dillinger and the Barker gang out of business. Almost at once in New Orleans, Kohn could see that the police corruption was the product of the Mafia crime boss Carlos Marcello, whose territory went beyond New Orleans and into Dallas, Mississippi, and parts of California, Mexico, and the Caribbean, including Cuba. Kohn's investigation led him to conclude that Joseph Civello, the Mafia street boss of Dallas, was a longstanding subordinate of Carlos Marcello. Civello was Marcello's boss of Dallas at the time of the "shootin' scrape" and had been since 1956.

In 1959, Kohn testified on his investigative findings about Carlos Marcello before the McClellan Committee. Its chief counsel Robert F. Kennedy, two years away from becoming his brother's attorney general in 1961, expressed appreciation to the crimefighter and made a vow to him: *"Mr. Kohn, I thank you very much...and I can assure you that, sooner or later, we will do something about Mr. Marcello. We cannot permit this kind of corruption to exist in the United States."*

That's the same Marcello that AG Kennedy would later kidnap without warning.

Carlos Marcello, in his turn before the McClellan Committee, refused to answer every single question put to him by chief counsel Kennedy.

In his well-researched and insightful book *Mafia Kingfish: Carlos Marcello and the Assassination of John F. Kennedy* (McGraw-Hill, 1988), author John H. Davis quotes Aaron Kohn that Marcello's criminal empire *"required, and had, corrupt collusion of public officials at every level including police, sheriffs...prosecutors, mayors, governors, judges...state legislators, and at least one member of Congress."* Marcello's home base was New Orleans, where he, his wife, his children, and his brothers lived. Marcello's legitimate businesses were in New Orleans, as was Congressman Hale Boggs's district. Aaron Kohn claimed that Representative Hale Boggs's biggest financial backer in his many elections to public office was Carlos Marcello.

Following my 2004 publication of *I Heard You Paint Houses*, I had occasion to speak by phone with the late Robert Maheu, a man whose 1975 Church Committee testimony about his actions in the Bay of Pigs conspiracy has much to do with suppressing the truth in Dallas. Maheu was a friend of my literary agent Frank Weimann, who arranged the telephone conversation. While my purpose in speaking with Maheu was not related to the Bay of Pigs Invasion, Maheu spontaneously expounded with great anger on the "murders" committed by the Kennedy brothers in their refusal to provide air support and cover to the "poor boys who were stranded defenseless on the beach waiting to be slaughtered." Maheu's emotion was still palpable over forty years after the "debacle." As we should know, the Bay of Pigs Invasion is almost always referred to as a "debacle."

At any rate, Maheu directed me to an aide named Karen who lived in Washington, DC. In an interview over dinner she told me that when Maheu, a former FBI agent, worked for the airline tycoon and billionaire Howard Hughes, Maheu on occasion would fly to New York with a suitcase full of cash that he would drop off at the Hotel Pierre on Fifth Avenue, where candidate Nixon and his attorney general, John Mitchell, then headquartered.

These were the times in which Carlos Marcello flourished and Hale Boggs made his political career. Is there any way the godfather of New Orleans failed to put a smile on all of his congressmen's faces?

Whether Congressman Boggs was on Marcello's donations list is impossible to corroborate at this late date, but at the very least, when President Johnson chose Boggs, he knew that Boggs and Marcello lived and operated in the same town legendary for its corruption.

And finally, at the end of that day, after twelve hours at his desk, President Johnson had the rubber stamp he needed to keep the Kennedy "aura" alive.

The key players on the seven-member commission were Ike's personal allies: Earl Warren and Allen Dulles. Both of them were appointed by Ike to their positions in the Supreme Court and the CIA at the same time. Several of the commissioners included three favorable to CIA covert operations, that is, clandestine undeclared warfare: Russell, Ford, and McCloy. The remaining two, Cooper and Boggs, were men who could be counted on politically.

The chairman was the only member with criminal law experience. As Warren explained in his memoirs: *"As District Attorney for a large metropolitan county for years, I personally prosecuted many murder cases and guided through my office scores of others."*

The earnest amateurs on the commission's legal staff couldn't stand a chance against a stacked deck and loaded dice.

With the exception of Arlen Specter, a former young assistant in the Philadelphia district attorney's office, the supporting legal staff was a group of lawyers with no criminal law experience.

As you'll see, the two members of the legal staff in charge of handling Jack Ruby innocently got themselves in a world of trouble with Earl Warren.

CHAPTER SEVENTEEN

Which Felony Murder?

Plausible deniability was the first rule of every CIA secret military operation, such as the 1953 CIA coup d'état that deposed the prime minister of Iran, Mohammad Mosaddegh.

Could this ten-year-old CIA intervention in Iran have been the "international complications" that could "come up to us" if President Johnson had not been "careful" in the creation of the commission? There certainly was more than enough felonious criminal activity in that Middle East coup to worry the American conspirators, such as Allen Dulles and Ike, as they turned over the CIA and the rest of the government to a new administration.

It wasn't until 2013 that the CIA finally admitted to orchestrating the riots for the coup d'état that had left three hundred dead by felony murder.

Essentially, felony murder is a crime that allows prosecutors to charge a conspirator in the commission of a felony with first-degree murder should even an unplanned death occur.

If you're part of the armed robbery conspiracy, you're part of the murder.

In the Warren report we shall see Earl Warren suppress multiple criminal conspiracies. Without the conspiracy there is no felony murder.

Every coup has at least one felony, such as holding a gun on someone. Another felony murder is the 1954 coup d'état of President Jacobo Arbenz of Guatemala.

Could this have been the "international complications?" Again, there certainly was more than enough felony murder activity to worry Allen Dulles and Ike. Ike had told his CIA men about to go forward in Guatemala, *"I want you all to be damn good and sure you succeed."*

Ike was glad to be told that this coup led to only one death, that of a courier. But one death is enough for a charge of felony murder.

Arbenz had distributed land belonging to the United Fruit Company to peasants. Meanwhile, Allen Dulles and his older brother, Ike's secretary of state John Foster Dulles, held substantial blocks of stock in the United Fruit Company. Warren commissioner John J. McCloy had served on its board of directors.

Allen Dulles had quite a résumé. Following Arbenz, the next coup in which Dulles's name appears was that of the Congo's prime minister, Patrice Lumumba, who fell to a firing squad in the last few days of the Eisenhower administration in January 1961.

In 1975, fifteen years after Lumumba's execution, the Senate finally held hearings on the CIA's role in plots to assassinate foreign leaders. One witness was President Eisenhower's note-taker for a meeting held prior to the Lumumba murder. The witness testified that Eisenhower's words "came across to me as an order for the assassination of Lumumba." Another said, "The president's statement came across as a great shock."

This murder does not appear to have been felony murder but merely a hit ordered by Ike and in need of suppression by Earl Warren.

Plausible deniability struck two more times in the spring of 1961. First came the felony murder case of the failed Bay of Pigs attack on Cuba by anti-Castro Cuban exiles on April 17, 1961. Then came the coup in the Dominican Republic that led to the death of dictator Generalissimo Rafael Trujillo.

Following Trujillo's death, plausible deniability was used again by President Kennedy and his administration twenty days before his own murder. This was designed to keep the Kennedy administration's hands clean in the November 2, 1963, kidnapping deaths of Prime Minister Ngo Dinh Diem of South Vietnam and his brother and chief advisor, Ngo Dinh Nhu. While the plan was not to murder the brothers, felony murder is often unplanned.

And so we know why AG Kennedy personally selected Dulles and McCloy behind the curtain: to cover up felony murder and the occasional hit.

Allen Dulles was strangely returned to the national scene on November 29, 1963, a little less than two years after he'd been forced to resign in disgrace by the Kennedys as a casualty of the strange debacle of the CIA-commanded Bay of Pigs Invasion.

Could this CIA intervention in Cuba have been the "international complications" that could "come up to us?" There certainly was more than enough felonious activity and death to make it the mother of all crimes.

As felonious as the other coups were, this strange debacle in Cuba was the one of most concern to those in the "CIA picture, you see," during Assassination Weekend and the torturous months to follow. This was Earl Warren's "only client."

If not "careful" it could have led step-by-step to first-degree murder charges against two presidents, Eisenhower and Kennedy.

And as will be proven, the Bay of Pigs Invasion did lead directly to the president's death, and to the carnage of that Friday through that Sunday.

CHAPTER EIGHTEEN

The Strange Debacle

As Dulles had served Ike in the 1960s U-2 debacle, immediately following the triple homicide in Dallas he was called upon to perform in the role of a suppressor of the truth in Dallas.

President Kennedy and Attorney General Kennedy had lots of experience with Allen Dulles within the first three months of the Kennedy administration in 1961, and all of it had been bad.

When Allen Dulles sat down on his Warren Commission chair in November 1963, he was the same man who in September 1961 had been fired by President Kennedy as the director of the CIA for his allegedly botched handling of the CIA's failed coup to overthrow Fidel Castro at the Bay of Pigs. That strange debacle was a disastrous two-day invasion of Cuba by fifteen hundred anti-Castro Cuban exiles, an invasion commanded, financed, planned, and supported by the United States. The exiles were trained by the CIA in Guatemala and shipped to a beach at the Bay of Pigs on the Caribbean island's south shore. Strangely, the invasion force attacked without air cover from a nearby aircraft carrier. American jets, the most advanced in the world, were parked a stone's throw away on the aircraft carrier

Essex, awaiting orders from President Kennedy, who seemed to be waiting for "word" of something himself before deciding what to do.

President Kennedy received news of the landing of the exiles shortly after midnight. Inexplicably, he did not authorize the jets, nor artillery support from the big guns of the seven destroyers also nearby, much less order the deployment of the ten thousand US Marines in striking distance waiting for orders.

The fifteen hundred Cuban exiles were pitted against two hundred thousand of Castro's soldiers and armed militiamen supported by Castro's thirty-six outdated warplanes, which could easily have been disposed of by the American jets had such a strike been ordered.

As exile leader Tony Varona, during his inspection of the exile training camp in Guatemala, put it to one of the CIA operatives planning the invasion: *"You'll have only a few hundred men. How can you win? Castro has two hundred thousand."*

Varona was told there'd be an air "umbrella" of jet planes protecting the invaders from Castro's forces.

At midnight a force of about fifteen hundred exiles launched without air cover to protect them from being slaughtered. As the horror unfolded on the beach, President Kennedy said, according to his White House aide Richard Goodwin: *"How could I have been so stupid? Why couldn't this have happened to James Bond?"*

Playing stupid was the president's plausible deniability for an "international complication" behind the scenes, but this was as serious as it gets.

Castro's soldiers and militia were unimpeded as they arrived at the front in buses, bringing heavy firepower to bear on the exiles that were stranded on the beach.

At that point President Kennedy ordered the *Essex* to move thirty miles farther out to sea. Step-by-step President Kennedy seemed to be backing out and making no effort to come to the rescue of those exiled freedom fighters, much less aid their cause of deposing the dictator Fidel Castro.

Four American pilots from the Alabama Air National Guard had seen enough of the slaughter. They boarded their planes and entered the battle on their own. After destroying some Cuban ground assets and making an attempt on Castro's headquarters, the Americans were shot down. Upon learning of that and comparing it to the U-2 incident and the pilot Francis Gary Powers, Robert F. Kennedy said to CIA Assistant Director Richard Bissell: *"This better not be another Francis Gary Powers. Those Americans better goddamned well be dead."*

On March 13, 1962, a year after the failed Bay of Pigs Invasion, the Joint Chiefs of Staff presented a memorandum to President Kennedy urging a "false flag" operation against Cuba called Operation Northwoods. Under the plan, acts of terrorism would be committed against the US by the US and blamed on Cuba as a prelude to the American conquest of Cuba.

President Kennedy rejected the proposal.

Back during the planning for the Bay of Pigs Invasion, AG Kennedy had heard Allen Dulles coldly warn the president that *"we have a disposal problem."* Dulles explained that the president couldn't afford to have exiles returning from this failure badmouthing President Kennedy as a pathetic weakling.

Regarding the "disposal problem," while President Kennedy waited for news from advisor Walt Rostow at the CIA command post, the president resolved to his aide that *"if we have to get rid of these men, it is much better to dump them in Cuba than in the United States."*

While President Kennedy was still waiting for word of some kind from Walt Rostow, the president cut back half of the previously ordered exile bombings of Castro's puny military airports. The president said to Richard Bissell about the bombing: *"I want it minimal."* Then the president canceled any further bombing of Castro's planes parked on the airfields, thereby enabling Castro's negligible air force to go airborne and dominate the skies.

In the last planning session before the launch of the exiles the president complained about the potential "noise level" of the exiles' bombing raids. The president strangely had become preoccupied with the quest for less noise.

At an event in Washington, DC, the night of that debacle, Jackie Kennedy swayed on the dance floor with Senator George Smathers, Democrat of Florida. Attorney General Kennedy cut in, took Smathers aside, and reported on the progress of the invasion: *"The shit has hit the fan. The thing has turned sour in a way you wouldn't believe."*

To begin with, the invasion was not the product of a declaration of war. America had no legal justification to participate in a conspiracy to plan and direct the operation. The deaths of Castro's people being bombed on the ground constituted premeditated first-degree murder. The deaths of the exiles constituted felony murder.

What was President Kennedy thinking of or feeling in his heart as reports kept coming in from Walt Rostow that the exile force of young men was being slaughtered?

Two years later when President Kennedy was slaughtered, it was Walt Rostow's brother Eugene, the dean of Yale Law School, who, unsolicited, came up with the idea of a rubber-stamp commission. Dean Eugene was his brother's keeper. The cover-up was to begin before Senator Eastland got a chance to ask Walt what he was waiting to hear at CIA Headquarters during the invasion. By 5:00 p.m. on April 19, 1961, the invasion that had started two days prior was over.

While "plausible deniability" was supposed to have been everyone's goal in this failed invasion to begin with, it was the furthest thing from a sneak attack and far more of a wide-open secret.

As author Peter Wyden quipped: *"The CIA's recruiting stations in Miami made the operation 'as secret as Christmas Day.'"*

At Dulles's forced retirement ceremony, President Kennedy unveiled the Biblical verse in the lobby of CIA headquarters for all time: *"And ye shall know the truth and the truth shall make you free."*

After the Bay of Pigs Invasion President Kennedy said he'd like to "splinter the CIA into a thousand pieces and scatter it into the winds."

Based on what the public knew at the time, one of those splinters would have been Allen Dulles.

No wonder Attorney General Kennedy had to make it appear as if President Johnson had picked Allen Dulles for the commission. The attorney general would have looked like the biggest fool on Earth if he had been exposed as the one selecting Dulles. But if they wanted a fixer, Dulles had the résumé.

When the invasion was all over, future President Richard Nixon advised President Kennedy: *"I would find proper legal cover and I would go in."*

That was an option that his abject failure had deprived President Kennedy of ever trying again. He'd had his turn at bat. He had knelt in the on-deck circle, got in the batter's box, and struck out on three called strikes. His bat had never left his shoulder.

There had to have been a lot more to the Bay of Pigs than the public was allowed to know.

What was the president up to? Had there been a congressional investigation of "Dallas" by Senator Eastland, it would have examined Cuba and Castro and this strange debacle. So much for the Kennedy "aura" if Senator Eastland and his staff had gotten their hands on the investigation of the triple homicide.

Nine days before the Bay of Pigs, Fidel Castro said in a speech: *"For months the [CIA] has been preparing on the soil of Guatemala… military bases and armies of mercenaries to attack our country…. When they place a foot here, they will learn the fury of the people who will fall upon them."*

On Saturday April 8, 1961, the day of that Castro speech, the CIA's project director for the invasion, Jake Esterline, and his CIA partner, Marine colonel Jack Hawkins, went to Assistant Director Richard Bissell's house to resign.

"This invasion makes no sense to us," said Esterline. *"If you do not abandon this plan, we are tendering our resignations here and now."*

Bissell replied, *"There will be an air umbrella."*

"If you don't want a disaster," said Colonel Hawkins, *"we absolutely must take out all of Castro's air force."*

"The president is committed to that," said Bissell. *"It will be done. Please trust the president on this."*

Esterline and Hawkins walked away from Bissell not entirely convinced but still on board.

CHAPTER NINETEEN

Bloody Anarchy

A s we know, the Bay of Pigs Invasion included a top-secret plot to assassinate Fidel Castro.

It was hatched by President Eisenhower; his CIA director, Allen Dulles; and his assistant director, Richard Bissell, and was executed by President Kennedy and conspired in by Attorney General Kennedy.

Although in 1975 during the Church hearings the CIA would confess to a conspiracy to murder Castro, in its day it was so secret that it had no code name. In my notes I use the acronym CONTAC, the "conspiracy to assassinate Castro," as distinguished from the later eight Operation Mongoose CIA plots to kill Castro that were in place until the day President Kennedy died. Those were personally managed by 007 aficionado Attorney General Robert Kennedy, the only attorney general known to have led a hit squad.

A top-secret 1967 inspector general report, initially concealed by the CIA, stated about Operation Mongoose: *"It is likely that at the very moment President Kennedy was shot a CIA officer was meeting with a Cuban agent in Paris and giving him an assassination device for use against Castro."*

On that same dreadful day, French journalist Jean Daniel met in Havana with Fidel Castro. More than once President Kennedy had used journalists to carry messages of goodwill to Communist leaders. This was one such occasion. During Daniel's interview of Castro, news came in that Kennedy had been assassinated. Castro got up and said, *"There goes your mission of peace."*

Unlike CONTAC, Attorney General Kennedy's Mongoose Operation was a murder conspiracy that did not include an invasion of Cuba, only plain first-degree murder. For well over two years the Kennedy brothers pursued the premeditated hit with a vengeance that was spawned by their Bay of Pigs humiliation.

In the summer of 1963, some few months before the president's assassination, the future secretary of Health, Education, and Welfare under President Johnson, Joseph Califano, was on a committee planning disruptive operations in Cuba. Califano said: *"Bobby Kennedy talked about knocking off Castro...I was stunned. He was talking so openly and there were other people in the room...knock off meant kill... no ifs, ands, or buts, no doubt."*

As for CONTAC, a murder around which the Bay of Pigs Invasion was built, former CIA director Richard Helms stated: *"Castro was supposed to be dead by the time the Exiles landed."*

In an interview by historian and author Michael Beschloss, Richard Bissell confirmed Richard Helms's statement: *"The assassination was intended to reinforce the plan. There was the thought that Castro would be dead before the landing."*

Senator George Smathers of Florida told Beschloss that President Kennedy told him that Castro would be "knocked off" before the exiles hit the beach at the Bay of Pigs.

Professor Arthur Schlesinger, Jr., confirmed both Richards of the CIA and the Florida senator in 1998: *"It should be pointed out that the assassination project was initially integral to the invasion scheme."*

Why wasn't Castro, as Bissell put it, "dead before the landing?" That Castro was not dead on arrival is what turned the invasion into such a debacle.

What did CONTAC look like when it was planned? Why did it go wrong?

Retired FBI agent, aide to billionaire Howard Hughes, and a private eye, the previously mentioned Robert Maheu was on a monthly CIA retainer for odd jobs. Maheu was a close friend of a Mafia made man named Johnny Roselli who had managed the Chicago family's Cuban casino before Castro took over all the Mafia's businesses in Cuba. The CIA, behaving as amateurs, asked Maheu to solicit Johnny Roselli to do a gangland hit on Castro for $150,000 with $25,000 down. Had these Ivy Leaguers known the first thing about the Mafia they never would have made such a proposal. The CIA didn't know Roselli was a made man because no one knew what a made man was until Joseph Valachi's congressional testimony.

According to Arthur Schlesinger, Jr., the assassination contract was presented to Maheu as "a necessary ingredient of the overall invasion plan." Maheu's CIA handler, James O'Connell, urged Maheu: *"If Fidel, his brother Raúl, and Che Guevara were assassinated thousands of lives might be saved."*

Maheu reflected, *"I'm no saint. I'm a religious man and I know that the CIA was talking about murder."*

While the CIA was plotting murder, Professor Schlesinger was advising the new president on the need for the correct ambassador to be installed in Cuba after the murder in order to, as he put it, "make sure that the new regime gets off on a socially progressive track."

The Harvard professor, a future Pulitzer Prize winner, advised the president on what covering falsehoods to tell if the invasion failed: *"We will have to be prepared to show that the alleged CIA personnel were errant idealists or soldiers of fortune working on their own."* The president must be shielded as "one of our greatest national resources.... When lies must be told [it must be] by subordinate officials."

Maheu was to observe, *"Not even in the movies would people believe that the United States government and organized crime were holding hands to remove a dictator from power."*

Johnny Roselli insisted that Maheu bring his CIA boss, James O'Connell, to the next sit-down, which Maheu did. The CIA, as amateurs, did not understand that exposing O'Connell to the Mafia gave the Mafia a live named person to use for blackmail if they ever needed it. James O'Connell's identity and role in the murder plot was a huge chip the Mafia could use to bargain with for sky's-the-limit Mafia adventures.

To the next sit-down Johnny Roselli brought his Chicago Mafia boss, Sam Giancana. On paper to the amateurs in the CIA, it looked like a natural. The Mafia bosses hated Castro for stealing all their Cuban casinos and other businesses. This was an opportunity for the Mafia to get that stolen property back.

As well, Giancana and President Kennedy saw eye to eye on certain human values. They were partners who shared the same mistress, the attractive Judith Campbell Exner. The 1975 Church Committee report identified her as a "close friend of President Kennedy [who had] frequent contact with the president from the end of 1960 through mid-1962. FBI reports and testimony demonstrate that the president's friend was also a close friend of John Roselli and Sam Giancana and saw them often during the same period."

By March 1962 Judith's love affair with President Kennedy was the subject of an internal FBI memo, which included a list of her frequent calls to the White House. J. Edgar Hoover got the material to President Kennedy at a private lunch. The president promptly broke up with his "friend" who had made seventy calls to the White House during the preceding year. In her memoir *My Story* (Grove Press, 1977), this former Jerry Lewis publicist wrote that Giancana once bragged to her about his indispensable 1960 election help to presidential candidate Senator John F. Kennedy: *"Listen, honey, if it wasn't for me your boyfriend wouldn't even be in the White House."*

Florida Mafia boss Santo Trafficante was picked up on a bug corroborating Giancana: *"We break our balls to get him elected and look what he does to us."*

Cuba was the territory belonging to Florida Mafia boss Santo Trafficante, and so Trafficante was brought into the CONTAC plan. At the final meeting, Johnny Roselli gave Trafficante odorless and tasteless botulism toxin poison pills he had received from James O'Connell. Trafficante was to give them to his Mafia hit man in Havana to dissolve into Castro's beverage for Castro to die speedily.

With Castro dead and an announcement to that effect made to the people of Cuba over the CIA's bogus Cuban radio station, the United States would have a pretext for an all-out invasion of Cuba using the extensive hardware sitting in the Caribbean parked near the Bay of Pigs waiting for the word of Castro's death from Walt Rostow at CIA Headquarters. The pretext for an outright American invasion of jet planes, naval bombardment, and US Marines would have been to protect the Americans still in Cuba, who would otherwise be caught in the middle of "bloody anarchy." With all the assembled hardware and personnel the American invasion would have lasted no time, and with Castro presumably killed by Cuban exiles, the Yankees on the march would have had plausible deniability.

To give evidentiary support for the pretext to invade Cuba on a mission to restore law and order, the CIA made up a memo for the file and planted it thirty-eight days before the invasion of April 17, 1961:

March 10, 1961

CIA Internal Information Report No. CS – 3/467, 630

Many people in Camaguey believe that the Castro regime is tottering and that the situation can at any moment degenerate into bloody anarchy...

Camagüey is one of Cuba's largest cities. It is found in the middle of the island en route to the Bay of Pigs. We know this is a planted and false memo because it lists no source, only a belief held by "many people" in Camagüey. It is self-serving gossip, not intelligence.

Further, it dramatically contradicts all contemporaneous legitimate intelligence about Cuba.

There was another memo placed in the file that same day of March 10, 1961. This one is sourced and reasoned. It comes from the CIA Board of National Estimates and says: *"...we see no signs that portend any serious threat to a regime which by now has established a formidable structure of control over the daily lives of the Cuban people."*

Castro had been killing his potential enemies daily, executing anyone who had worked for any part of the former Batista government, including menial laborers.

The invasion was not a harebrained plot. It was a brilliant plan by some highly intelligent planners, however amateurish and gullible they were in *affaires de Mafia*.

It would have worked easily and smoothly if only the Mafia, using untraceable fast-acting pills, had succeeded in murdering Castro. Not hearing news of Castro's assassination from Walt Rostow, President Kennedy had no choice but to slowly dim the green light and turn it to red.

President Kennedy was no weakling; he was a PT-109 war hero, brainy enough to know the "international complications" that would "come up to us" if he had proceeded with a blatant American invasion of Cuba without plausible deniability. By sucker punching Cuba without cause, the president would be violating the United Nations Charter, the American laws that created the CIA and the National Security Council, and the treaty that created the Organization of American States. Because treaties require Senate approval, all treaties are the law of the American voters.

As well, the president would be violating US laws against murder and conspiracy to murder. The murder conspiracy planning with two Mafia bosses, Sam Giancana and Santo Trafficante, and well-known Mafia figure Johnny Roselli, was done in front of witnesses like Maheu and O'Connell. It had been planned in public places in Florida, in suites at two hotels; in California at the Brown Derby; in

New York at the Fifth Avenue Plaza Hotel; and in Washington, DC, at the White House.

Nothing doing but that President Kennedy needed to stage a rescue of Americans and designate his attack as a peace mission once Castro was poisoned to death by anti-Castro Cubans.

But why wasn't Castro dead? Was this another U-2 Francis Gary Powers fiasco?

Maheu said to the Church Committee in 1975 that "perhaps" the hit man had gotten "cold feet." EFW tells us that by his use of the word "perhaps" Maheu is offering up a suggested cover story. Johnny Roselli also gave the Mafia's cover story when he claimed to the Church Committee that the hit man "lost his nerve."

As Joe Pistone and Lin DeVecchio taught me, there is no such thing as getting "cold feet" or "losing your nerve" when a Mafia boss gives you an order to kill. You do as told or your designated murder victim is just as dead and you're dead too.

You get "cold feet" when your godfather Santo Trafficante tells you to go get some cold feet, and you "lose your nerve" when your godfather Sam Giancana tells you to go lose your nerve.

The Mafia had turned this green light to red. At this point I rushed to my research files.

Eagerly, I went through my notes on Attorney General Kennedy's kidnapping of Santo Trafficante's closest friend, Carlos Marcello, looking for the date.

Marcello was kidnapped, cuffed, abused, and dragged to Guatemala on April 4, 1961. The Bay of Pigs landing began on April 17, 1961, thirteen days after the kidnapping of Carlos Marcello.

At the moment of the Bay of Pigs Invasion Carlos Marcello was stumbling around in Guatemala protecting his ribs from further injury while the Mafia was trying to get him home to his family.

Is it possible that Attorney General Kennedy didn't think about the two-year-old CONTAC conspiracy with the Mafia the moment he heard his brother had been assassinated and less than an instant before he ran to Earl Warren for help and selected Dulles and

McCloy to cover up all the Mafia murder conspiracies? The attorney general had learned all about felony murder and first-degree murder in law school.

The worst consequence of the Bay of Pigs is that the Mafia now knew they had Robert F. Kennedy by the throat and could squeeze any time.

Who could imagine that after the cuffs were put on an unsuspecting Carlos Marcello on April 4, 1961, the Mafia would still attempt to do business with the Kennedys some thirteen days later?

When CONTAC began as a CIA mission under Ike many months earlier, the Mafia had no reason to distrust him. During the campaign of 1960 the Mafia was on John F. Kennedy's side and had no reason to distrust him, either, at least until he designated his younger brother as attorney general.

Had the Mafia allowed CONTAC to succeed, it would have catapulted President Kennedy and his brother into astonishing glory in the voters' eyes for both freeing Cuba from communism and ridding the world of Castro. This is glory that would ensure the president's reelection and allow him to keep his brother in his position, driving a stake in the Mafia's heart until Robert F. Kennedy reaped his own glory from using Joe Valachi in trial after trial against the Mafia. Robert F. Kennedy would then run for president and win in a landslide in 1968.

The huge bonus for these Mafia planners by far is that they now had a blackmail grip of Robert F. Kennedy's throat, with live and credible witnesses. Additionally, they had restaurant and hotel receipts, and likely candid Mafia photographs at each CONTAC meeting location, to corroborate the Kennedy administration's conspiracy with the Mafia to commit a first-degree murder of Fidel Castro.

The biggest bonus for the Mafia by far from its participation in CONTAC is that the Mafia knew it now had a license to kill President Kennedy, and to get away with it, as G. Robert Blakey would publicly declare in the aftermath of his report for the House Select

Committee on Assassinations. The Mafia killed President Kennedy and "got away with it," Blakey often stated.

The Mafia bosses knew that Robert F. Kennedy would have to be extremely "careful" and remain silent in the face of his brother's assassination or face a murder investigation by Senator Eastland.

Robert F. Kennedy would have to do whatever his Mafia blackmailers told him to do. The attorney general and his staff would have to lay off the Mafia at once, or Robert F. Kennedy would be facing charges of solicitation to murder, conspiracy to murder, first-degree murder, and felony murder.

Most importantly, Robert F. Kennedy would have to end his anti-Mafia crusade.

At the outset, the Mafia certainly would want Joe Valachi to be fired from his work for the Department of Justice. And he was. There would be no more public testimony before Congress. One previously scheduled minor court testimony involving Valachi would go to trial, but then no more. Valachi was told the deal was off, and he was sent to solitary confinement. This hero of the moment would linger in jail. He became depressed and tried to hang himself with a wire from his radio, but he weighed too much and failed in his attempt.

In the beginning, during the honeymoon period, Valachi was encouraged by AG Kennedy to make notes of all he could remember about his life, with an eye toward a book to be published.

Nicholas deBelleville Katzenbach was Attorney General Kennedy's righthand man. When President Kennedy was assassinated, Katzenbach ordered Joseph Valachi to discontinue his notes. He would not be allowed to write his book. The Mafia's chokehold on Robert F. Kennedy was in place, and they wanted no more from this Mafia traitor. Valachi and his professional writer protested. Katzenbach sued Valachi to halt publication. Then it was settled. Valachi could write a book, but it had to be told in third person, not in the more-truthful-sounding first person.

William G. Hundley, chief of the organized crime section of AG Kennedy's DOJ, was poolside at Kennedy's house in Hickory Hill

93

when the call came in to the attorney general from J. Edgar Hoover that the president had been shot and was dead. Hundley was there to attend strategy meetings in AG Kennedy's all-out war on the Mafia.

Hundley reported: *"The minute that bullet hit Jack Kennedy's head it was all over. Right then. The organized crime program just stopped."*

G. Robert Blakey gave voice to Robert Kennedy's dynamic role before his brother's assassination: *"He gave us a whole feeling of electricity to what we were doing. We thought we were the New Untouchables."* And they were.

Robert F. Kennedy continued to hold the title of attorney general; that way no anti-Mafia assistant or staffer could pick up where he had left off. Things would remain in limbo with his foot on the brake until the titular attorney general successfully ran for the United States Senate from New York in 1964 and was replaced as attorney general by Ramsey Clark, a lawyer whose father, Supreme Court Justice Tom Clark, wrote the anti-police decision in *Mapp v. Ohio* for Earl Warren, creating the exclusionary rule of the criminal law revolution. Ramsey Clark opposed even legal wiretapping. He could be counted on never to approve a tap or a bug, counted on to withhold his necessary signature, as long as he was the attorney general.

But Robert F. Kennedy and his team's courageous war on organized crime was over on November 22, 1963, with the Mafia winning the war.

Another organized crime fighter present at poolside discussing strategy was Manhattan US Attorney Robert Morgenthau. *"I saw him often after that,"* Morgenthau said, about the attorney general, *"but he never mentioned organized crime to me again."*

In 1962, a year after Marcello's kidnapping and a year before Valachi's testimony, Carlos Marcello had regaled a guest named Edward Becker at Marcello's hunting and fishing property, Churchill Farms. Becker was a publicist for the Chicago outfit's Riviera Hotel and Casino in Las Vegas. According to author John H. Davis, Becker asked Marcello: *"Man, isn't it a fuckin' shame the bad deal you're getting from Bobby Kennedy? I've been reading about it in the papers. All that deportation stuff. What are you goin' to do about it, Carlos?"*

"In Sicily if you want to kill a dog, you don't cut off the tail...but if the dog's head is cut off, the dog will die, tail and all."

Marcello explained to Becker that killing Robert F. Kennedy would bring vengeance from President Kennedy, but killing President Kennedy would be the end of every bit of Robert F. Kennedy's power. Marcello explained the way they do in Sicily is to get a "nut."

As we know from his attempt to kill former General Walker, to get Oswald as the "nut" in 1963, all the Mafia had to do was tell him about CONTAC and show him some corroborative exhibits from Johnny Roselli's blackmail kit: hotel and restaurant receipts, clippings of accounts of Castro speeches about America's plans to assassinate him, newspaper accounts of Marcello being abused in Guatemala by Attorney General Kennedy in 1961, photos secretly taken, Marcello's IRS lien, and show him the pills that were meant for Castro. All they had to do was befriend him, assure him that they would fly him away to a safe house in a safe country. Make him feel a part of the mission.

Urging liquidation of Castro got General Walker a half-inch away from being picked off through his window by the same rifle used to kill the president.

CHAPTER TWENTY

Cops and Robbers

Having done his best to preserve the Kennedy "aura," President Johnson turned his tape-recording attention to covering his own butt and blackmailing Robert F. Kennedy in the process.

"I attended one meetin'," said President Johnson about his entire tenure as vice president, *"and they asked me my opinion, and I said if you boys want to play cops and robbers, why don't you get on television?"*

President Johnson's comment was made in a secret White House telephone conversation on February 1, 1964. At the time of the call, the Warren Commission was starting its second month and was still two days away from taking a word of testimony.

The president's comment about "cops and robbers" was referring to a "meetin'" held six months earlier about a covert conspiracy among the CIA, President John F. Kennedy, the Attorney General Robert F. Kennedy, and their Ivy League advisors. The operation approved at the "meetin'" over Johnson's "cops and robbers" objection was to result in two felony murder deaths on foreign soil.

"But goddammit," Johnson continued on tape, *"let's don't go doing it with allies..."*

"You're right," responded Sargent Shriver, who was at that moment the late President Kennedy's first director of the Peace Corps.

Why would President Johnson say something that top-secret on White House tape to Sargent Shriver? Shriver was not just a Kennedy political loyalist, he was married to Eunice Kennedy Shriver. At the time of this conversation Eunice was imminently due with the Shrivers' fourth child. They would have five children together, including television reporter Maria Shriver. Sargent Shriver's marriage to Eunice made him the brother-in-law of both Robert F. Kennedy and of the recently assassinated president.

In his role in setting up and heading the Peace Corps, Shriver had had nothing to do with "international complications." He was not anywhere near that August 31, 1963, "meetin'," yet he was able to respond, *"You're right."* Shriver understood exactly what Johnson was saying and that it incriminated both the late president and the current attorney general, his wife's brothers. Shriver needed no explanations. He even understood the puzzling sentence, *"Let's don't go doing it with allies…"*

And Johnson precisely understood that Shriver, who didn't know he'd been taped, would repeat to Johnson's rival and enemy Robert F. Kennedy everything Johnson had said. Johnson's words were a warning to the very popular Robert F. Kennedy.

"But they wanted to play cops and robbers," Johnson added, *"and they have."* Johnson closed with: *"…anyway, that's water over the dam."*

And it would remain so unless some word or deed by Robert F. Kennedy that displeased President Johnson caused the dam to spring a leak.

This secret tape, in addition to shooting one across the bow of Robert F. Kennedy, also provided President Johnson with some butt covering. He was only ever at one "meetin'" and he had opposed the plot.

The plot on tape that February 1, 1964, was the November 2, 1963, arrest-turned- assassination of Ngo Dinh Diem, the president of South Vietnam, and his chief adviser and brother, Ngo Dinh Nhu.

They were kidnapped, blindfolded, and shot in their heads Mafia-style in the Catholic church where the two Vietnamese leaders had sought sanctuary.

Five days after the Diem assassinations, the United States fulfilled a promise it had made to the killers as incentive for a coup, that if Diem were to be overthrown, the United States would recognize the new regime.

"Overthrow" includes the felony of kidnapping, which the Kennedy administration authorized, and the unauthorized murder in the church that followed means felony murder charges for all involved.

Vietnam then descended into a series of unstable governments. There were eight successive military regimes.

On February 1, 1966, discussing on tape how South Vietnam got started on a downhill spiral, President Johnson said to United States general Maxwell Taylor, after whom Robert F. Kennedy's youngest son Maxwell Taylor Kennedy is named:

"They started out and said we got to kill Diem because he's no damn good, and let's knock him off. And we did."

Taylor replied: *"That's where it all started."*

Johnson said, voice rising: *"That's exactly where it started. And I just plead with 'em at the time. Please don't do it. But that's where it started, and they knocked him off."*

Later that same day on tape President Johnson said to future anti-Vietnam War candidate for the Democratic nomination for president, Senator Eugene McCarthy, about the Diem and Nhu hits: *"We all got together and got a goddamn…bunch of thugs and we went in and we assassinated [Diem]."*

The motive for the Kennedy administration turning against Diem was what politicians call bad press. Buddhist monks in South Vietnam were protesting the Catholic Diem's administration by setting themselves on fire. At a Buddhist monk demonstration, Diem's soldiers opened fire, killing nine monks.

Johnson viewed Diem as the "Churchill of Asia." Johnson had hung a portrait of the late Diem in the White House, rubbing it in. Senator and future presidential nominee Hubert Humphrey passed that portrait four days after Kennedy's assassination. Johnson said to Humphrey: *"We had a hand in killing him. Now it's happening here."*

The next day Johnson said to Kennedy White House assistant Ralph Dungan: *"I want to tell you why Kennedy died, divine retribution…divine retribution. He murdered Diem and then he got it himself."*

Lyndon Johnson seemed to be relentless in letting Robert F. Kennedy know that his future in politics depended on Johnson's silence.

That week in the White House Blue Room, President Johnson spoke directly to Robert F. Kennedy and said: *"The United States is getting a bad name around the world."*

Portly Pierre Salinger was President Kennedy's press secretary, a visible symbol of all that the Kennedy administration had stood for. Johnson let loose to Salinger on the day following the verbal carpet bombing of Sargent Shriver: *"Sometimes I think that when you remember the assassination of Trujillo and the assassination of Diem, what happened to Kennedy may have been divine retribution."*

To his credit, Robert F. Kennedy had voted "no" on the Diem brothers' coup d'état, but he did nothing to stop it along the way. As a lawyer, he had a legal and ethical duty to blow the whistle and stop the coup as a crime in progress. As attorney general he had more than a double duty.

Earl Warren had his work cut out for him in keeping a lid on all this if certain friends, colleagues, and political allies of his were to avoid jail and if he were to be their hero for life.

Meanwhile, what was President Kennedy's grand strategy for South Vietnam, obviously a strategy that included getting rid of the Diem regime?

Pulitzer Prize–winning journalist Charlie Bartlett was so close to his friend Jack Kennedy that Bartlett had played matchmaker and introduced Jack to Jackie.

Before the Diem coup, President Kennedy revealed his grand strategy to Bartlett: *"Charlie, I can't let Vietnam go to the communists and then go and ask these people—the voters of America—to reelect me. Somehow, we've got to hold that territory through the 1964 election."* At the same time, the president said the same thing to Democratic senator Mike Mansfield, to White House advisor and historian John Kenneth Galbraith, and to the Canadian prime minister Lester Pearson. In plain English he said to each of his esteemed friends to let the slaughter of American soldiers, sailors, and Marines continue until Election Day in November 1964.

CHAPTER TWENTY-ONE

Man Hunt

Before America's entry into World War II in 1941, a Fritz Lang movie entitled *Man Hunt* was released. It stood for the proposition that Adolph Hitler should have been assassinated prior to starting the war by joining Russia in attacking and conquering Poland in 1939.

In *Man Hunt*, Walter Pidgeon played the role of a big game hunter who set out with his high-powered rifle and scope to track down Hitler at his lair.

After the war there was a general consensus that unimaginable horror and suffering could have been prevented worldwide had someone assassinated Hitler early on.

According to historian Peter Grose in his biography of Allen Dulles, *Gentleman Spy*, a few years before becoming director of the CIA Allen Dulles declared to an audience that *"Assassination may be the only means left of overthrowing a modern tyrant."*

In his memoirs, Earl Warren revealed that President Eisenhower was a warrior inclined toward approving assassinations of pro-communist leaders. In January 1965 on their flight to Winston Churchill's funeral in London, Ike criticized Warren for rulings that he thought were soft on communism. Warren asked Ike: *"What would you do with communists in America?"*

Without hesitating, Ike replied: *"I would kill the S.O.B.s."*

General Eisenhower had been a witness to communist treachery even after the Russians and the Americans had become allies against the Nazis. Advancing from the east as the war was ending, the Red Army had driven the Nazis to within forty-five miles of Warsaw, Poland. By radio, Stalin encouraged the Polish resistance in Warsaw to stage a revolt against the Nazis. Expecting Russia to continue its successful advance, the poorly armed Polish resistance came out of the underground and attacked the heavily armed Nazis from within. It was a trap set by Stalin. No match for the Nazis in the Warsaw uprising, the Polish resistance was decimated. Ike and Churchill sought to help the Polish resistance with air power, but after their raids the Allied planes would need to land on Russian-held territory, which Stalin refused to allow. Stalin's plan was to let the Nazis eliminate those largely anti-communist Poles in the Polish resistance so that communism would dominate Poland after the war.

At the start of the war in 1939, Ike watched the Russians split Poland with the Nazis and massacre twenty-two thousand Polish people.

After the war, Ike watched American communists pass nuclear weapons secrets to the Soviets, thereby starting the Cold War, then watched Stalin start the Korean War.

Indeed, Ike "would kill the S.O.B.s."

Castro's early fabrication to President Eisenhower that he was pro-democracy, when all the while he was planning a communist dictatorship, rankled Ike, and so in 1960 Ike felt justification in approving the *Man Hunt* killing of Castro in CONTAC.

Oswald's attempt on the life of General Walker was a *Man Hunt* shooting.

In his report, Earl Warren wrote about Marina Oswald's *Man Hunt* argument with her husband: *"She testified that Oswald said that General Walker was a very bad man, that he was a fascist, that he was the leader of a fascist organization, and when I said that even though all of that might be true, just the same he had no right to take his life, her husband said if someone had killed Hitler in time it would have saved many lives."*

The updated version of the big game hunter in *Man Hunt* was the fictional hero James Bond 007, the British spy with a license to kill, a license that Oswald acted as if he had.

In his biography *Robert Kennedy: His Life* (Simon & Schuster, 2000), Evan Thomas observed that in the CIA "the Kennedys were pleased to find real life James Bonds."

No wonder Robert F. Kennedy was to throw himself into the many Operation Mongoose plans to assassinate Castro, to knock him off.

CHAPTER TWENTY-TWO

The Lone Nut Books

When the Warren Commission got underway, Robert F. Kennedy's first selection after Warren, the historically disgraced Allen Dulles, a man of well-known "international complications," immediately demonstrated how to manipulate the amateurs in the room. In the first meeting of the commission Dulles passed out a book to each individual present. It was a study of American presidential assassinations and attempted assassinations. The book demonstrated that each assassin was a "lone nut," a "lone cowboy." When one of the commissioners, John J. McCloy, ever keeping up appearances, protested that Abraham Lincoln's assassin, John Wilkes Booth, had been part of a conspiracy, he was shot down by Dulles, who claimed that Booth was a "nut" and that he so dominated the assassination that he was for all intents and purposes a "lone nut" assassin.

Had a professional homicide detective been handed such a book at such a meeting, the detective would have asked, "Were any of these lone-nut killers in your book shot dead in less than forty-eight hours by another lone-nut killer?"

Of course, this propaganda in support of the "lone nut" concept was being passed out before the commission had lifted a finger to investigate anything. Every member receiving such a book was politically astute enough to be aware of that. Jurors deliberate after a trial, not before. Quickly or slowly, each amateur at the table had to realize that this book being handed out on the first day was essentially marching orders. It was handed out with the approval of Chairman Warren, who was sitting there allowing it to be done. It had to have been coming down from President Johnson, who had earlier told each of these commissioners that J. Edgar Hoover's FBI already was prepared to supply a finished report that would agree with this "lone nut" book.

"You'll find a pattern running through here that I think we'll find in the present case," Dulles said.

As they looked at their chairman for guidance, what did the commissioners already know about him? What information about him stood out in their minds when he looked in their eyes and told them: *"We have only one client, the truth."*

Was it his internment of the Japanese? His extortion of Ike to become chief justice? His elevator conspiracy? At any rate, they certainly knew he was not somebody in Washington, DC, whom one defied.

They might not have known why or how, but distribution of the book confirmed what they had to already know—there was a fix of some kind brewing, one they were about to become a part of.

CHAPTER TWENTY-THREE

A Shoddy Piece

Two professional and prominent investigators and Mafia-savvy people, qualified experts on the secret world of the Mafia, Robert F. Kennedy and one of his principal Mafia fighters, Professor G. Robert Blakey of Notre Dame, each, after much study, had concluded that the Mafia killed President John F. Kennedy.

As noted, Blakey would go on to distinguish himself as the chief counsel to the 1976–1979 House Select Committee on Assassinations. Blakey was to be an FBI hero in the 1980s for having drafted legislation that legalized wiretapping and bugging under certain circumstances; for creating the RICO statute that made it virtually illegal to be a member of the Mafia, thereby enabling the prosecution of previously untouchable Mafia bosses, such as those on the Mafia Ruling Commission; and for expanding the use of the Witness Protection Program. Blakey's innovations led directly to the Mafia Commission case narrated in *We're Going to Win This Thing* (Berkeley, 2011) by Lin DeVecchio and me.

In 1976 Congress had established Blakey's House Select Committee on Assassinations. This was a year after the private Zapruder film of the assassination was televised in 1975 by my

Brooklyn Law School classmate Geraldo Rivera. The select committee was formed to restudy the assassinations of President John F. Kennedy and the Reverend Martin Luther King, Jr., in an effort to clear up some of the inconsistencies for the voting public.

As noted, Professor Blakey had said publicly over the years that he believed the Mafia "killed Kennedy and got away with it." Blakey believed it even though the committee for which he was chief counsel was not able to gather any evidence to make such a specific finding.

As to President Kennedy's assassination, Professor Blakey's committee relied on expert acoustical evidence of the sound made by a fourth gunshot, which led to a conclusion that President Kennedy had been killed as the result of a generic conspiracy but not a provable Mafia conspiracy.

Professor Blakey's committee's proof for their generic conspiracy was based on the fact that Oswald's sniper's nest of boxes of books on the sixth floor of the Texas School Book Depository revealed three empty cartridge shells, not four. And it was only three empty cartridges that were heard to hit the plywood floor immediately below according to witnesses on the fifth floor within earshot, who were shaken by the high-powered weapon being fired above them three times, not four.

After investigation, the select committee agreed with the Warren Commission that Oswald had fired those three shots and that, therefore, it had to have been someone else who had fired the fourth shot from somewhere else and with a different rifle.

This fourth shot supposedly missed everything, and the bullet was never located. When the Blakey Committee released its report in 1979, the sound made by a fourth bullet that missed everything seemed to be clear proof of a conspiracy but not one that necessarily included the Mafia. According to the committee's report, dictation equipment was found to have picked up from an open microphone on a Dallas police officer's motorcycle the sound of a fourth gunshot. *Voilà!*

However, this acoustical evidence was discredited fairly quickly. Practically since the day the select committee announced its final report in 1979, all other experts examining the dictation equipment have found it to contain no sound of the firing of a weapon or any sound remotely like a gunshot. Furthermore, the Dallas motorcycle officer was identified and explained where he had been during the assassination. There could not have been a gunshot sound at his location.

As for the often-discussed second shooter at the grassy knoll, no proof of such a shooter was ever uncovered. That shooter would have to have been out of his mind to begin shooting after Oswald had first shot three times. Oswald's shots would have instantly put law enforcement and spectators on high alert. There could be no guarantee in advance that the grassy knoll and the area just below it wouldn't be crawling with potential eyewitnesses, unlike the sixth floor of the book depository building, which was then being renovated and not likely to have anyone but the assassin on it. No grassy-knoll assassin could predict what unpredictable reactions of evasion would emanate from the Secret Service, the Dallas PD, or the driver of the president's limo. There would be no efficient sniper's nest, no adequate cover provided by the grassy knoll's fence. A shooter with a rifle would have been too exposed.

Speaking as a lawyer who has tried whiplash or flexion-extension injury cases, the fact that on the bullet's impact the president's head whipped backward is meaningless. No cars in those days had headrests. The back support of a car's front seats didn't reach as high as a passenger or driver's shoulders. All the mechanisms for a rear-ender type of whiplash reaction of the neck and head were in place the instant the brain was hit and died, rendering the neck muscles limp. The limo was moving forward with the back support of his seat pushing the president's back forward while leaving the head behind on a lifeless neck, a classic whiplash. Let someone slap your back and you will feel that your head wants to travel backward while your back moves forward, only slightly, because not being brain-dead, your muscles are functioning.

On October 31, 1963, Peter Magaddino, a capo in his father's Magaddino crime family of Buffalo, New York, a family on the Mafia Commission, was heard on illegal electronic surveillance regarding President Kennedy around the time of the Valachi hearings a month prior to the assassination: *"They should kill the whole family, the mother and father, too."* Many miles away in a separate illegal bug of the Bruno family of Philadelphia, boss Angelo Bruno was tape-recorded regarding both Kennedys: *"We ought to whack the big one...the little one."*

As he had approved a tap on Martin Luther King, Jr., Attorney General Kennedy had approved the illegal Magaddino and Bruno family interceptions, but the attorney general never mentioned the Mafia electronic intercepts or their threatening contents to the Warren Commission.

In fact, Robert F. Kennedy chose not to try to help solve his brother's murder, that of Officer Tippit, or of Lee Harvey Oswald by not allowing himself to be questioned to see what might "come up to us."

In 2012 on the *Charlie Rose* television show before Rose got caught exposing himself, Robert F. Kennedy's eldest son, Robert F. Kennedy, Jr., said that both he and his late father believed the Mafia had killed President Kennedy.

Robert F. Kennedy, Jr., said that his father judged the Warren Commission report to be a *"shoddy piece of craftsmanship.... He publicly supported the Warren Commission report, but privately he was dismissive of it."* The younger Kennedy explained, *"He was a very meticulous attorney. He had gone over reports himself. He was an expert at examining issues and searching for the truth."*

Charlie Rose asked whether Robert F. Kennedy, Sr., had "some sense of guilt because he thought there might have been a link between his aggressive efforts against organized crime" and John F. Kennedy's assassination. Robert F. Kennedy, Jr., answered: "I think that's true. He talked about that." Robert F. Kennedy, Jr., went on to point out that Jack Ruby's phone records "were like an inventory" of organized crime figures.

In 1967 Robert F. Kennedy, Sr., told his brother's former White House advisor Richard Goodwin that he believed Carlos Marcello, "the guy from New Orleans," had assassinated his brother.

In 1967, with a presidential election coming up in 1968, President Johnson was still lobbing stray shots at Robert F. Kennedy. This can be seen by a tape-recorded conversation President Johnson conducted with speechwriter Leo Janos.

Johnson said to the speechwriter: *"I never thought Oswald acted alone. I can accept that he pulled the trigger."*

President Johnson added that when he inherited the presidency, he found that *"we had been operating a Murder Inc. in the Caribbean."* Both Castro and Trujillo would fulfill that description.

Howard K. Smith was one of the most prominent broadcasters of any era. Around that same time, President Johnson said to Smith: *"I'll tell you something that will rock you. Kennedy was trying to get to Castro, but Castro got him first."*

CHAPTER TWENTY-FOUR

Felony Murder in Delaware

In wading through the many "Dallas" books, I kept encountering a Warren loyalist book called *Case Closed* (Anchor, 2013) written by lawyer and investigative journalist Gerald Posner, who seemed to be on every Dallas documentary. Posner's was among the first books I read after digesting the Warren Commission report.

By virtue of his ignoring the key evidence regarding Oswald's plan of escape and the equally key evidence of Ruby's intentional lies, Posner concluded that Chairman Warren got it right: that Oswald had acted alone, as if he were indeed a lone-wolf assassin, and that Jack Ruby's killing of Oswald was a lone-wolf murder, not motivated by a conspiracy. Posner had found himself a niche, posing as the rational man in a field full of conspiracy theories.

Posner followed Warren's strategy of minimizing the existence and materiality of the key eyewitness to a conspiracy, Mrs. Earlene Roberts. Posner reduced her testimony to a dismissive footnote. Without explaining in any way, he brazenly and briefly stated that "her account was false." Without providing evidence, Posner cited a science editor who agreed with him, but this science editor earlier had admitted that he had made up a false story for his newspaper that Oswald had been a paid FBI informant. Posner left out of the footnote any reference to that made-up story, which had spread the world over. Nor was there any mention of the fact that this science editor that Posner had solely relied on in a mere footnote also had admitted to posing as FBI agent James Hosty to obtain Hosty's personal phone bills.

In *Case Closed*, there was not a single mention of felony murder or of the Bay of Pigs Invasion.

If a lawyer like Posner tackles the triple homicide in Dallas and doesn't mention the intricacies of felony murder in Cuba, he has no means of understanding and unlocking the Warren cover-up designed to protect at least these five felony murderers: President Dwight D. Eisenhower, Attorney General Robert F. Kennedy, CIA Director Allen Dulles, Assistant CIA Director Richard Bissell, and President John F. Kennedy—and his "aura."

What kind of investigative reporter, I wondered, buries evidence and relies on another writer who fabricates evidence?

Following my reading of *Case Closed*, I scratched the surface of Posner's internet biography to find that in 2010 he had lost his chief investigative reporter's job at the *Daily Beast* on the grounds that a number of his articles contained outright plagiarism. A reporter for Slate.com, Jack Shafer, had uncovered Posner's plagiarism. For his *Daily Beast* articles Posner had stolen from an article in the *Miami Herald*, a *Miami Herald* blog, a *Miami Herald* editorial, a *Texas Lawyer* magazine article, and a health care journalism blog.

Spurred on by these findings, the *Miami New Times* did an investigation that led to uncovering plagiarism from a variety of sources in three of Posner's nonfiction books and uncovering numerous examples of quote falsification. In one headline he was dubbed "Super Plagiarist."

This author of one of the bibles of Warren Commission loyalists, Mr. *Case Closed*, had found a substitute for thinking called stealing.

As a lawyer adept at plagiarism, perhaps Posner never really learned the felony-murder rule or how to use it. Many legal commentators today believe the rule should be abolished. Some countries like Canada, England, and Ireland already have abolished it as too harsh a punishment for a nonshooter.

Prosecutors often show leniency to felony murderers. Almost as soon as a real felony murderer, a pro boxer named Bobby Golson, was sentenced in 1976, first to "hang by the neck until dead," and then to "life with no chance of parole," even though he possessed no gun in the liquor store armed robbery that went wrong, my co-prosecutor Peter Bosch, State Police detective Jimmy Corrigan, and I had decided that we would keep an eye on Bobby Golson in jail. If he proved himself to be a model prisoner, because of his crying remorse and spontaneous confession when he was arrested for the robbery and felony murder of schoolteacher Philip Whiteman, who doubled as a liquor store clerk to support his family, we would consider going to bat for Bobby and back a commutation that would give him an ordinary life sentence, making him eligible for parole someday.

That didn't mean he'd get parole, but at least he'd be allowed to apply after serving a normal life sentence.

In the beginning, Warden Redman at the Smyrna prison would tell me: *"Charlie, Bobby is just a big baby boy who can't keep his mouth shut. It keeps getting him in trouble."*

And so we stayed in the background, and I concentrated on building my medical malpractice law career. As time went on, reports on Bobby showed growth and maturity. One day I got a call from a prison counselor who knew about my meetings with the warden and my inquiries about Bobby over the years.

"Charlie," he said, *"Bobby Golson has really straightened himself out. We're backing his commutation. We're proud of his efforts. We know he didn't even have a gun."*

"Bobby's father has taken an interest in him and it's really helped a lot with Bobby's outlook and maturity," the public defender said when I called him to follow up.

It was music to my ears.

"Peter, Jimmy, and I saw Bobby as a big boy in search of a father," I told the public defender. *"He thought he'd found it in his Muslim fight manager Clarence X Hooks."*

"Bobby lost contact with his father as a toddler. The influence of his father's new interest in him now has really helped Bobby grow. His father's a jazz musician and Bobby is very proud of that."

I was blown away by this revelation.

"Are you talking about the jazz icon Benny Golson? Benny Golson can't be Bobby Golson's father."

"Yes, he is. Do you know him?"

"Every jazz fan knows him. I have some of his records. My buddies and I played one of his records to death in college, Killer Joe. *I wish I'd known this at the time. We might have been able to use his father to persuade Bobby to testify for us and save himself. But Bobby, a Muslim recruit at the time of the murder, was afraid of the Muslims in jail."*

"Well, his father wasn't in his life then anyway."

I drove down to the prison and met with Bobby Golson. He had already served about twenty years and still felt remorse in his soul all these years later for the unintended death of the schoolteacher and liquor store clerk, Philip Whiteman. While the Muslim ringleader had a gun, Bobby acted as an unarmed lookout, wearing a paper bag with eyeholes, keeping an eye outside the store. As of now the ringleader and shooter, who was twenty-two at the time, has served over forty years. His bid for a commutation has been hampered by a 1976 jailbreak.

As an aside, through my interrogation of one of the captured escapees, and with the help of my two investigators, Steve Simmons and Larry Dunkelberger, we located Philip Whiteman's shooter and the shooter's partner under a porch. Bobby had nothing to do with the prison break.

Elated, I called Peter Bosch, living out west, and Jimmy Corrigan, working as an investigator for a law firm, and we agreed to write a letter signed by the three of us in support of Bobby's commutation.

Later, in a separate proceeding before the Parole Board, Bobby was paroled after twenty years in prison.

Years later, the shooter I'll call Dexter X established a career from the Smyrna prison writing detective mysteries featuring black characters. He was also designated one of President George H. W. Bush's Thousand Points of Light for his work teaching illiterate prisoners to read. Felony murder is still a serious crime in Delaware, but there can be leniency along the way.

Bobby's father Benny Golson had a featured role, playing himself, in Steven Spielberg's movie *The Terminal* starring Tom Hanks.

When Benny called to tell me that the great director had asked him to be in the film, I asked Benny, *"What will you be playing?"*

"I told you," Benny said, *"I'll be playing myself."*

"No, I mean, what tune will you be playing?"

"Oh, 'Killer Joe.'"

It was my collegiate soundtrack.

CHAPTER TWENTY-FIVE

Which Marble Palace?

Before being sent to prison, Frank Ragano, Esq., was a well-known Mafia defense lawyer who had represented Jimmy Hoffa, Carlos Marcello, and Santo Trafficante.

Many years prior to my decision to try to unlock the mysteries of "Dallas" and to analyze the Warren Commission report, when I saw Frank Ragano interviewed on television in 1994, I believed his statement that his client Jimmy Hoffa in 1963 had asked Ragano to deliver a message to two of Ragano's other clients, Florida/Cuba Mafia boss Santo Trafficante, and Dallas/New Orleans Mafia boss Carlos Marcello.

In promoting his book *Mob Lawyer* (Scribner, 1994), Frank Ragano repeated on television what he had told his author, Selwyn Raab: that Hoffa wanted Marcello and Trafficante to hurry up and "kill that son-of-a-bitch John Kennedy." Ragano's simple tale and his voice and demeanor in front of the camera while recounting Hoffa's request had the ring of truth, at least in my perspective. Ragano had the look of a man remembering an incident, not reciting from a script he'd memorized. He had the look of truth-telling that interrogators learn to recognize the more successful interrogations and cross-examinations that they do.

Ragano said Hoffa's request had been made in Jimmy Hoffa's Teamsters headquarters in Washington, DC, while they were working on trial preparation.

This assassination solicitation happened on Tuesday, July 23, 1963, four months before President Kennedy was assassinated. Ragano claimed to have been meeting with Hoffa about new indictments that had recently been handed down and said that Hoffa was beside himself with rage. According to Ragano, Jimmy Hoffa told him: *"Something has to be done. The time has come for your friend and Carlos to get rid of him, kill that son-of-a-bitch John Kennedy. This has got to be done. Be sure to tell them what I said. No more fucking around. We're running out of time—something has to be done."*

As I used to teach young policemen, the more scrupulously honest you are in your everyday life, the easier it is to recognize lying when you hear it and see it.

That Hoffa made this request, I knew, didn't mean that the Mafia killed President Kennedy because Hoffa had urged the Mafia to do so. Knowing how the Mafia works, it had its own menu of reasons for the assassination, and it is much more likely that Hoffa was allowed to believe that the Mafia had done "Dallas" for him, and therefore he owed the Mafia for it.

Before setting out on my new adventure into the mysteries of the triple homicide in Dallas, I felt I'd better take a look at how one of the most authoritative defenders of the Warren Commission report handled Frank Ragano's allegation of a message from Hoffa, an allegation made by Ragano almost thirty years after the three murders.

The late Vincent Bugliosi, the esteemed Manson Family prosecutor and the author of *Helter Skelter: The True Story of the Manson Murders* (W.W. Norton & Company, 1994) wrote a 1,612-page book on President Kennedy's assassination called *Reclaiming History* (W. W. Norton & Company, 2007). It was twice as long as Earl Warren's report. A CD-ROM full of footnotes came with it, totaling another

1,028 pages. Vincent Bugliosi agreed with Warren that Jack Ruby and Lee Harvey Oswald were not co-conspirators. Bugliosi reached this conclusion after having read all twenty-six-appendix volumes to Earl Warren's report. Bugliosi had no doubt and firmly believed that there was no evidence of any conspiracy, Mafia or otherwise.

Bugliosi established himself as a supreme Earl Warren loyalist, alongside Gerald Posner.

But cutting into the diamond, how did Bugliosi deal with the unmistakable evidence of conspiracy contained in the message Hoffa had asked Ragano to deliver? I looked up Ragano in the index. Bugliosi challenged the factual basis for certain other things Frank Ragano claimed in his book, such as deathbed comments he claimed Trafficante made to him. Maybe Ragano did lie about those certain other things to puff up his book sales, maybe not. But I never heard Ragano speak any words or sentences on television on these other subjects. These other subjects were printed on a page. All I cared about was the televised verbal statement that I saw and heard. His testimony had the ring of truth to this cross-examiner. I fully believed that Frank Ragano delivered the message from Jimmy Hoffa to "kill that son-of-a-bitch John Kennedy."

On page 1,181 it appeared that Bugliosi, the jury trial lawyer, agreed with my assessment of Ragano. Bugliosi pointed out that the details of lawyer Frank Ragano's allegation in that regard did, in Bugliosi's own words, "smack of the truth." Bugliosi certainly had the experience to make an assessment like that. Frank Ragano and Jimmy Hoffa had been meeting to strategize for an upcoming criminal trial against Jimmy Hoffa brought by Attorney General Kennedy's "Get Hoffa Squad."

But then, according to Vincent Bugliosi, Frank Ragano self-destructed. Ragano, Bugliosi argued, was unable to keep his story straight about the important matter of the physical location of his trial preparation meeting with Hoffa. Bugliosi charged Ragano with contradicting himself as to the physical location of the conversation that Bugliosi felt had the "smack of the truth."

According to Bugliosi, the first time around Ragano said his conversation with Hoffa, in which Ragano was asked to deliver a message to Marcello and Trafficante took place, in Bugliosi's words, "in the executive dining room of the Marble Palace Hotel in Washington, DC."

Bugliosi went on to chastise Ragano and wrote:

"In November of 1992, Ragano told essentially the same story to a national audience in a Frontline *TV special, but he said the conversation took place not in the Marble Palace Hotel, but in Jimmy Hoffa's office at the Teamsters headquarters in Washington, D.C. Marble Palace Hotel? Jimmy's office? Better make up your mind, Frankie."*

Frankie?

Staring at the page that contained this analysis I knew at once that at least this much of Vincent Bugliosi's book was not authoritative. There is no Marble Palace Hotel in Washington, DC, nor as far as I know, anywhere in the country. The Marble Palace and the Teamsters headquarters building are one and the same place. The Teamsters headquarters building is named the Marble Palace. The only other building called the Marble Palace in Washington, DC, is the prestigious Supreme Court building.

As to criticizing this statement by Ragano, Bugliosi needed to be infinitely more careful, if for no other reason than that it is universally accepted that Louisiana Teamster Ed Partin, an undercover informant for Attorney General Kennedy's prosecution of Jimmy Hoffa, recounted a similar story to the Department of Justice about Jimmy Hoffa having announced to Ed Partin, in Hoffa's Teamsters headquarters office, that he wanted a Kennedy killed soon. But Hoffa's intended assassination victim was Robert F. Kennedy. Hoffa told Partin he wanted someone to shoot Attorney General Kennedy with a high-powered rifle while Kennedy drove his Cadillac convertible to and from his office with the top down, as was AG Kennedy's custom. This conversation took place well prior to President Kennedy's assassination by use of a high-powered rifle as he rode in a convertible Lincoln with the top down in Dallas.

Hoffa told Partin, *"I've got to do something about that son of a bitch Bobby Kennedy."*

Ed Partin became the star witness in Attorney General Kennedy's first successful prosecution of Jimmy Hoffa that finally put Hoffa in Lewisburg federal prison, setting off the chain of events that ultimately cost Jimmy Hoffa his life. The late Vincent Bugliosi had no business writing about Frank Ragano without taking the esteemed Ed Partin into consideration.

That Ragano reported on television and in his book practically the same words Partin reported to the Get Hoffa Squad is corroboration of Ragano's testimony that Bugliosi disparaged. Bugliosi's failure to deal with the heroic Ed Partin was unacceptable.

Among my qualifications to give a thumbs-down to Warren loyalists like Bugliosi and Posner, whose nonfiction books blindly parrot the details and conclusions of the Warren report, is that I am also a professional fiction writer. Fiction provides a new way to understand facts and issues. In *The Right to Remain Silent* I exposed the devastating effects that Chief Justice Earl Warren had had on police work, especially in the field of interrogation. The novel was based on homicides I solved through the interrogation of suspects whose fingers I managed to keep from the *Miranda* mute button, "lawyering up." It was a successful novel, and its theme was well understood.

President Ronald Reagan praised my efforts in an August 11, 1988, unsolicited letter to me: *"I commend your novel...for your forthright stand on improving the protection of law-abiding citizens."*

The Warren report, as the saying goes, was not going to be the first police report or FBI 302 I ever read.

While this "Marble Palace" mistake does not mean that the respected trial lawyer and author, the late Vincent Bugliosi, didn't know what he was talking about, as a rule state prosecutors have little to no experience with the Mafia. I got mine from mingling with experts and from my writing experiences with Frank "The Irishman" Sheeran, Joe Pistone, Lin DeVecchio, and the New Untouchables.

I gained a great deal of knowledge about the Mafia and about the Kennedy brothers' interaction with the Mafia, enough to understand what would motivate Jimmy Hoffa to ask Ed Partin to kill Robert F. Kennedy and to ask Frank Ragano to solicit Carlos Marcello and Santo Trafficante to kill President Kennedy.

CHAPTER TWENTY-SIX

Oswald's Motive

Proof of motive is not a requirement of the criminal law. It is a time-honored Rule of Evidence that makes proof of motive admissible in a criminal trial to strengthen the prosecutor's evidence of guilt in certain cases.

Shortly after President Kennedy's assassination, Attorney General Kennedy's right-hand man, Nicholas Katzenbach, sent a memo to President Johnson concerning Lee Harvey Oswald's motive. It stated: *"Speculation about Oswald's motivation ought to be cut off."* End of discussion. That's one way to unsolve a murder case.

Talk of Oswald's motive could lead to talk of a Mafia role in recruiting Oswald. As a "nut." Obviously, as Robert F. Kennedy's right hand, Katzenbach knew Mafia leaks could send his boss and his accomplices to jail for their roles in CONTAC in one big ka-boom.

However, as a former homicide prosecutor, Chairman Warren knew he could not avoid the subject of Oswald's motive altogether. Every law student learns MOM: motive, opportunity, and means. It is the acronym for proving a murder by circumstantial evidence. Here, Warren was staring at a gusher of both direct and circumstantial evidence in these cases of murder by Oswald and Ruby in all three respects of MOM.

Warren couldn't completely ignore Oswald's motive, just as the commissioners, especially McCloy, felt they had to appear to be conducting an investigation and could not get away with merely rubber-stamping Hoover's five-volume report that the FBI took all of seventeen days to prepare. Some mention of Oswald's motive, however slight, had to be made by Warren.

Jack Ruby had made Warren's task easier in stating a motive for Ruby's killing of Oswald by expressing a few trial-balloon motives that Warren could latch on to in his report.

As for Oswald, Chairman Warren was hereby instructed to "cut off" any motive talk. On page twenty-two of his report Warren said of Oswald's motive: *"...the commission cannot make any definitive determination of Oswald's motive."*

Employing EFW, the word "definitive" pops out of the box. Using his methodology on the page, Warren listed all of Jack Ruby's offered motivations, however speculative or laughable. As for Oswald, Warren cleverly injected the standard of proof to be "definitive." We see that definitive means a conclusive, final, decisive, ultimate, absolute, and complete motivation of Oswald.

Just in case we needed it drummed into our skulls, on page 423 of his report Warren returned to the subject of how stymied the commissioners were when it came to expressing even a single one of Oswald's many admissible motives. On that page Warren proclaimed: *"Many factors were undoubtedly involved in Oswald's motivation for the assassination; and the commission does not believe it can ascribe to him any one motive or group of motives."*

Let's just state the obvious; killers often have more than one motive, and each one is admissible.

John Wilkes Booth hated Lincoln, loved the Confederacy, loved the South, loved slavery, and believed the war had not ended with Lee's surrender to Grant. Likely, as an actor, his dramatic flourish after shooting Lincoln was motivated by the ham within.

If we handed out notebooks and conducted a pop quiz right now on Oswald's motives, the following true facts would be acceptable to any homicide detective's scenario:

Oswald had a volatile personality and was a staunch defender and worshipper of Fidel Castro.

Oswald tried to kill General Walker because Walker had given a speech urging that Castro should be "liquidated." Oswald bought his two guns right after Walker's threatening speech.

President Kennedy was a well-known hater of Castro and of communism. While Oswald presumably did not know about CONTAC or Operation Mongoose, he certainly knew of the Bay of Pigs Invasion to at least overthrow Castro, if not kill him.

A month before Oswald moved to Dallas, Fidel Castro publicly threatened that he would retaliate "in kind" if America made an attempt to assassinate him. Castro said to an AP reporter: *"United States leaders who plan on eliminating Cuban leaders should not think that they are themselves safe. We are prepared to answer in kind."*

And so, Nicholas, is this what needs to be cut off?

Fidel Castro later explained this comment to the Blakey Committee. Castro said that he had heard rumors that his life was in jeopardy from the Kennedy administration and he wanted President Kennedy to understand that an assassination plot against him could "backfire" on President Kennedy. As a footnote, Chairman Warren never attempted to interview Castro, but Blakey and Cornwell flew to Cuba to do so, and Castro cooperated.

In 1967, with Robert Kennedy now a United States senator from New York with his gaze tilting toward a run at the White House, and as rumors of CONTAC and Operation Mongoose began to seep out, likely from President Johnson, the political columnist Jack Anderson, a Johnson ally, reported that *"President Johnson is sitting on a political H-bomb—an unconfirmed report that Senator Robert Kennedy may have approved an assassination plot [against Castro] which then possibly backfired against his late brother."*

Jack Anderson's H-bomb revelation came to him directly from Johnny Roselli's personal attorney, clearly a warning to Robert F. Kennedy from the Mafia.

That was the time of President Johnson's "Murder Inc." remark, the start of a rumor, to speechwriter Leo Janos. In coordination with Jack Anderson's "H-bomb" column, President Johnson asked Director J. Edgar Hoover to prepare a top-secret report on what Anderson had reported. When finished, the FBI report was headlined: "Central Intelligence Agency's Intentions to Send Hoodlums to Cuba to Assassinate Castro."

In 1967 Robert F. Kennedy had much better poll numbers than Johnson, and it was taken for granted that Senator Kennedy would challenge Johnson in 1968.

CHAPTER TWENTY-SEVEN

Scarecrow

Before the killings, the FBI already had firsthand experience with Oswald's dangerous volatility and could have used that experience with Oswald to prevent all of the murders.

As was its duty, after giving the Oswald family a chance to get settled in America, the Dallas FBI office opened a national security investigation file. The last agent to work the investigation in Dallas was Special Agent James P. Hosty, Jr., a supporter and admirer of President Kennedy.

Initially in his security investigation of Oswald, Hosty treated Oswald as if he posed no danger in America. And then came bloody murder let loose.

J. Edgar Hoover promptly found Hosty's security investigation to have been negligent. Hoover disciplined the agent, giving him ninety days' probation. Hoover wrote to Special Agent Hosty: *"It has been determined that your recent handling of a security-type case was grossly inadequate...in view of the information developed concerning the subject of the investigation, it should have been apparent to you that he required a status which would have insured further investigative attention."*

The FBI brass kept Hoover's discipline of his negligent agent a secret and suppressed the whole episode. Director J. Edgar Hoover lied when he testified before the Warren Commission that the special agent in charge of the Oswald security investigation had done nothing wrong.

By then, the Bureau had already covered up evidence of Special Agent Hosty's slipshod handling of Oswald.

First, to conceal evidence that Oswald had a personality whose volatility should have been taken seriously as a threat to the president, and whose presence on the motorcade route should have been reported to the Secret Service, the Bureau removed from its files a note written by Oswald threatening to blow up the Dallas FBI office.

It was a note Oswald had written to Agent Hosty, who was investigating him. Oswald had delivered the threatening handwritten note to the Dallas FBI office on November 12, 1963, ten days before the assassination.

Second, the Bureau ripped up the only copy of the threatening note and flushed it down the toilet.

Third, the Bureau doctored Oswald's personal address book by purging Special Agent Hosty's name and address from it.

The Bureau later confessed to all these unpunished crimes around the time of the 1975 Church Committee.

After the FBI's confession, were voters supposed to trust any of the FBI's words and deeds, such as the FBI's interpretation of its July 18, 1964, so-called "passed" polygraph of Jack Ruby?

In 1976, a year after the 1975 FBI confessions to perjury and evidence tampering, the House Select Committee on Assassinations convened. G. Robert Blakey's committee put together a panel of the country's leading polygraph examiners to review the Warren Commission's 1964 polygraph charts of Jack Ruby. The esteemed members of the panel determined they were unable to interpret the examination because there were "numerous procedural errors."

I worked on formulating questions on many polygraphs with our polygraph operator Steve Simmons. There is no excuse for a single "procedural error." In 1976 the 1964 polygraph was not able to be read and interpreted, while the FBI operators in 1964 falsely claimed they were readable and showed no deception by Jack Ruby.

Because Oswald's bomb-threatening note to Hosty no longer exists, to know what it said we have the word of the receptionist who accepted it for Special Agent Hosty. The receptionist was Mrs Nannie Lee Fenner. She said Oswald "had a wild look in his eyes" when he delivered the note.

Mrs. Fenner had no motive to lie about the contents of the note, but Hosty did. Had he gone back to confront Oswald that fall, he could have spooked Oswald the way, as chief deputy, I had spooked a courthouse jailbreak and gun sale in 1976.

We had gotten word from an informant that Judy Shabazz Johnson, the wife of a radical murder defendant, was going to buy guns from a Wilmington gangster named Squeaky Saunders to use for a courtroom breakout. The crime was catching on among radicals, such as George Jackson of the Black Panther Soledad Brothers, who filled a courtroom with carnage in 1970 when guns were smuggled in to him during a murder trial. Ironically, it was a trial of California's version of felony murder.

After questioning the informant, his handler believed him. But we all knew that because of the criminal law revolution, we couldn't pick up Judy Shabazz Johnson and Squeaky Saunders for questioning. They both had lawyers. What made matters worse is that in those days we had no metal detectors or video cameras protecting the courtroom. I left the meeting with the informant on the gun sale to go to an unrelated meeting on another murder with a judge on the third floor, where our trial of the radical murder defendant was taking place. The first thing I saw upon reaching the third floor, sitting on a bench in the grand hallway under the courthouse dome, was Judy Shabazz Johnson and Squeaky Saunders. She was dressed in her flowing garb that could easily conceal a small arsenal. I walked directly to them as if I were looking for them, hovering in front of them a few inches away. Squeaky, in his black leather jacket, looked up at me and said "pshaw" as if to tell me he wasn't going to sell this woman any guns, at least not anymore. Judy looked down at the floor. We remained in this standoff until Squeaky shrugged and implored with his hands that he'd like to leave. I made room for him and then followed him down the three flights, staying five steps behind him. Twice he stopped, turned, and shook his head "no" to reaffirm that he had no intention of doing business with these radicals. He was a businessman, suspected bank robber, and murderer. I followed him out of the courthouse.

He made a right and headed to the East Side where Wilmington had produced one of the greatest jazz trumpeters of all time, the late Clifford Brown, and was now producing murderers.

Later that morning the Wilmington police borrowed a metal detector and an operator from the federal building and put up two video cameras high on a ledge. These cameras were just scarecrows, like the ones dressed up in musty old clothes that my grandfather Luigi DiMarco had used to scare birds from his crops in Staten Island. These cameras were not even hooked up to electricity because we had none at the height of the only useable ledge.

Had Hosty alerted the Secret Service to Oswald's note threatening a bombing, a note that was clearly the product of an unstable mind, the Secret Service would have more than spooked Oswald. This was the era prior to Chief Justice Warren's *Miranda* decision by three years. The Secret Service and the FBI legally would have picked up Oswald for questioning. That simple move would have spooked the President Kennedy assassination plotters and put the entire operation out of business, just the way Squeaky Saunders was spooked thirteen years later and put out of business. How sad to think how easy it would have been to keep our president alive in Dallas had Hosty simply done his duty.

To cover himself, Agent Hosty tried to minimize the violent and threatening nature of Oswald's note, claiming that it complained about Hosty visiting his wife, Marina, at her residence when Oswald wasn't there, no mention of a bomb threat. Hosty maintained that the note Oswald delivered to the FBI office said, in effect, "If you want to talk to me, you should talk to me to my face. Stop harassing my wife, and stop trying to ask her about me. You have no right to harass her."

Hosty added: *"After reading the note, I had tossed it in my file drawer at the office and not given it another thought. That is, not until November 22...."*

According to the testimony of the Dallas FBI office supervisor Gordon Shanklin about the contents of the destroyed note: *"I understand that there is a discrepancy in what Mrs. [Nannie Lee] Fenner says about what was in the note, and what Mr. Hosty says. In Mrs. Fenner's version, there is a threat to blow up the Dallas office and the Dallas field office...."*

Ka-boom.

These bombings happen. In 1920, Italian "bloody" anarchists had blown up a horse and wagon full of nuts and bolts on the corner of Wall Street and Broad.

Sorry, Gordon Shanklin, but because you're the one who told Hosty to destroy Oswald's note, and because Hosty ripped it up and flushed it down the toilet, it is Nannie Lee Fenner who gets to say what was in the note and not you or your law-breaking FBI agent.

Twelve years later when Mrs. Fenner was called to testify before the Church Committee in 1975 she stuck to her guns. The note was "a threat to blow up" offices of the FBI by a communist who had a "wild look in his eyes."

Evidence of Oswald's volatility, especially on the subject of Castro, and his attempt to kill Walker added credibility to his obvious motive to kill President Kennedy to protect Fidel Castro from assassination plots by President Kennedy.

In January 1975, twelve years later, Senator Church of Idaho made it clear just how bad of an "H-bomb" these Kennedy brothers' 007 plots had been: *"It is intolerable that any agency of the United States may engage in murder."*

As the FBI worked on their triple-homicide report for seventeen days and committed federal crimes that men have gone to jail for, the FBI brass was acting in its own self-interest. Just how volatile Oswald's personality was, admittedly, was suppressed by the FBI.

The other police agency Earl Warren relied on was the Dallas Police Department. In the wake of all the bloodshed, Jack Ruby's partner in his Vegas Club, Joe Bonds, testified that Ruby "made women available" to Dallas policemen.

Chairman Warren's report was forced to admit, because all the Dallas press knew it to be true, but without exploring its tremendous evidentiary value even a little bit: *"Ruby was known to have a wide acquaintanceship with Dallas policemen and to seek their favor."* Not a word more was said by Warren about this issue involving the brazen televised murderer of Lee Harvey Oswald in the basement of the Dallas police building. Not a syllable was uttered.

This was a relationship with Ruby that the Dallas PD had to view as dirty laundry, not all of it fit for all to see. Policemen have an expression for one caught in the middle of this well-known phenomenon: "Shit flows downhill."

Every policeman who knew Jack Ruby would be inclined to minimize his contacts with Ruby after he killed Oswald.

Yet some contacts can't be minimized. The very .38 Ruby used on Oswald was registered to a Dallas PD detective named Joe Cody. Cody bought it in his own name for Ruby so as to swindle Texas out of its tax on gun purchases, a tax waived for policemen.

CHAPTER TWENTY-EIGHT

Unlocking the Secrets of Dallas

In the course of nearly four decades as a jury trial lawyer I found that the keys to unlocking a mysterious case, criminal or civil, are sometimes tiny and not very shiny.

This is not the case in these three murder cases and related cover-up.

During my first reading of the Warren Commission report the keys jumped out at me as if from a jack-in-the-box. They made my jaw drop then, and they still do. The keys were gigantic and as bright as if made of neon lighting. There did not need to be conspiracy theories. Ever. Certainty was just below the surface.

About a third of the way through the Warren Commission report I saw plainly that there are separate questions to two dead men, Lee Harvey Oswald and Jack Ruby. Their obvious answers are the two giant keys to unlocking this triple homicide. They are the incontrovertible keys to corroborating that there was a conspiracy involving the Mafia to assassinate President Kennedy and a cover-up to hide any trace of that conspiracy.

These separate questions are:

1. Lee Harvey Oswald, where did you think you were going immediately after your assassination of President Kennedy and until your capture in a movie theater with a .38 in your hand? What was your escape plan? Quo vadis, Lee Harvey Oswald? Whither goest? Where were you going on foot?

2. Jack Ruby, why did you lie about every single one of your activities immediately following the assassination of President Kennedy and until the night before you executed Lee Harvey Oswald on Sunday morning? Why did you tell fifteen easily disproven lies about your whereabouts from 1:30 p.m. on Friday, November 22, 1963, until 7:00 p.m. on Saturday, the 23rd? Didn't you realize that your nose was growing with each brazen falsehood?

CHAPTER TWENTY-NINE

Quo Vadis?

Winding down his rubber-stamp report, Warren wrote: *"Finally, investigation has produced no evidence that Oswald had prearranged plans for a means to leave Dallas after the assassination, or that any other person was to have provided him assistance in hiding or departing the city."*

Quo vadis is Latin for "whither goest."

"Where are you going?" Saint Peter is said to have asked Jesus. When applied to Oswald, this question is the first of the two large keys to the truth in the evidence locker of a Dallas Mafia conspiracy.

Analyzing where Oswald was headed after he laid down his rifle on the sixth floor leads to a trail of evidence that proves beyond any doubt that Oswald did not expect to be heading to jail in eighty-eight minutes. Just as he had expected to escape from the General Walker shooting, Oswald had expected to escape from the President Kennedy shooting. He expected help from two Dallas police officers to escape. And help is the heartbeat of conspiracy—the aiding and the abetting.

To begin with, Oswald had chosen not to kill the president at the most efficient moment for a shooter, that is, when the presidential limousine convertible with the top down slowed to a crawl, almost standing still directly beneath the sixth-floor window of 411 Elm Street, as the limousine made an agonizingly slow left turn that was practically a U-turn. It would have been an easy ambush, straight down at a slowly approaching target getting larger and larger as it came crawling toward Oswald. His heart pumping and his Italian rifle at the ready beside him, he sat in the sixth-floor window as if an onlooker among countless others.

Snatching up his rifle at the exact moment he needed it and firing at that approaching target twenty yards away would have ensured that Oswald hit the president's head. For a mortal wound he'd have needed only one shot from a rifle at that distance. As the limo approached at a crawl it would have provided the president's heart as an easy additional kill target. The heart was not easily available in the rear shots Oswald had chosen. As the limousine made its turn, President Kennedy's profile, for an easy headshot, was on Oswald's side of Elm Street.

However, each of these easy shots would have meant there would be no escape for Oswald who was, as he had told *The Militant* communist magazine, "ready for anything."

Instead, Oswald planned to fire long distance from way behind the limousine after it had passed beneath him. It was a target getting smaller and smaller, with only the head available, and not the president's heart. The advantage to Oswald was that shooting at a distance from the rear meant that the eyes of the Secret Service agents in the vehicle directly behind the president's limousine would have been focused to the front. The agents would have had their backs to Oswald and to his rifle barrel starting to peek out the sixth-floor window. Oswald had sacrificed accuracy for the chance of escape.

He missed the moving limousine completely with his first shot.

Unlike John Hinckley, Jr., who sauntered up to President Reagan firing away at point-blank range, or Jack Ruby who darted out at Oswald firing at close range, Oswald intended not to get caught. His choice of a fading target supports that intent. Oswald passed up close range for long range, large target for small, a target slowed to a snail's pace by a hairpin turn for a moving target. He made these target choices for only one reason, simply so he could escape. But to where, Oswald? Quo vadis?

The Warren Commission refers to what happened next under a section Chairman Warren has entitled, "Oswald's Escape," agreeing to that limited extent, but without analysis, that Oswald was in the process of escaping when an hour and a half later he was arrested. In other words, his plan had potential. It had given Oswald an hour and a half head start.

In order for the elevator on the sixth floor of the book depository building to function, the elevator door on the first floor had to be closed for safety. It had not been closed despite Oswald's earlier request of a coworker who was leaving to watch the motorcade. Following his final rifle shot from his sniper's nest, and without an elevator, Oswald had to walk calmly down four flights to the second-floor cafeteria. There he got a Coke. A Dallas policeman hurried in and asked Oswald to identify himself. Oswald's supervisor told the officer that Oswald was an employee. That satisfied the officer, and Oswald casually strolled out of the building. He boarded a bus for the neighborhood of his rooming house by knocking on the bus door to stop the bus, even though it was not a bus stop. That way he wouldn't have to wait for the next bus. But traffic due to the assassination made the bus too slow for whatever Oswald had in mind. The bus was at a standstill. Oswald later admitted under pre-*Miranda* interrogation that he had left the slow-moving bus and taken a cab to his rooming house. He had the cab driver go to 500 North Beckley Street, over-shooting his address of 1026 North Beckley Street by a few blocks to deceive the cab driver. This lie about where he lived is again evidence of Oswald's intent to escape, his flight being a confession of guilt as if it were a signed confession.

The next eyewitness to see Oswald was the key witness to a conspiracy. Mrs. Earlene Roberts, the housekeeper for the rooming house where Oswald lived, would have been the star witness of any incisive investigation. It was 1:00 p.m., a half-hour after Oswald had shot President Kennedy at 12:30 p.m. Dallas time. Earlene Roberts said Oswald was in an unusually great hurry when he abruptly rushed into the house, "all but running," at 1:00 p.m.

"Oh, you are in a hurry," Earlene Roberts said to Oswald, according to testimony.

He reportedly flew past her without answering, rushed up to his room to quickly change his trousers, get a jacket, and grab his .38-caliber revolver. Altering his outerwear changed his appearance and constitutes additional relevant evidence that he intended an escape—yet another admission of guilt, the equivalent of a confession.

Oswald rushed out of the house in as big a hurry leaving as he had been when he arrived. What was that hurry? It was a hurry that had made him abandon his bus and switch to a cab—on his way to where? Where was Oswald going in such a hurry when he rushed out of the rooming house after just rushing in? Was he anxious to get busy wandering the streets of his Oak Cliff neighborhood aimlessly, as Chairman Warren leaves on the table as his only explanation? Or was he "all but running" to keep a rendezvous with those he believed would help him escape? His Plan A? Oswald didn't need help to get to his rooming house, but he desperately needed it once he got there.

Glaring evidence of a conspiracy was right before the seven commissioners, and so they closed their eyes and asked us all over the world to do the same.

Before he rushed out of the house, while Oswald was changing his clothes, Earlene Roberts saw and heard the telltale event in his escape plan. On page 253 of his report, Earl Warren states: *"The possibility that accomplices aided Oswald in connection with his escape was suggested by the testimony of Earlene Roberts...."*

Hooray! And to think, I doubted Earl Warren.

Chairman Warren reported that before Oswald left his room, Earlene Roberts heard a car horn beeping "several times." Mrs. Roberts looked out and saw that the beeping car was a marked Dallas police car with two officers in it. The police car drove slowly by the front of the rooming house, stopped momentarily in front of it, beeping its horn, then drove away. Oswald, who would have heard the same beeping that Earlene Roberts heard, came dashing out of his room ignoring the housekeeper, in as big a hurry to get out as he had been to get in.

Oswald rushed out headlong, apparently without fear of whatever he might encounter.

The time was 1:00 p.m. In the fifteen minutes between 12:45 p.m. and 1:00 p.m. there were three police radio car broadcasts describing the president's assassin, giving a general description that fit the slender Oswald: *"Attention all squads…the suspect…an unknown white male, approximately thirty, slender build, height five feet ten inches, weight one hundred sixty-five pounds."*

Dallas patrol cars normally contained one officer. Earlene Roberts knew this and knew her neighborhood's regular officer by sight. He was not in this police car. She saw their faces but didn't recognize either the driver or the passenger. She knew the car that normally patrolled her area to be number 170. This wasn't 170. Purposefully not identifying the following information as corroboration of Earlene Roberts's testimony, and mentioning it only in passing, Earl Warren inadvertently corroborated her by declaring that number 170 had been sold months earlier and the number not put back into service. Therefore, Earlene Roberts was correct in noting that the beeping police car was not number 170.

So here we have a corroborated eyewitness. Earlene Roberts said the beeping police car was not car number 170 and that testimony was proven to be correct by the prior sale of car 170.

Earlene Roberts attempted to guess at the car's number, a common occurrence among eyewitnesses trying to help, unless they are appropriately stopped. They need to be told not to guess. However, her guesses were remarkably similar: 106, 107, and 207, each with a zero in second position. But these three cars were accounted for, according to Dallas PD.

Chairman Warren used Earlene Roberts's attempts to help as an excuse to dismiss what she had seen. He chose not to investigate, analyze, or discuss in any way her detailed testimony about the several conspiratorial actions of the patrol car and Oswald's dashing out following its beeping and pulling away.

A former law enforcement officer, Warren suggested no scenario to explain the beeping police car that Earlene Roberts had seen with her own eyes and heard with her own ears.

Chairman Warren eagerly ran from the subject and used as an excuse the Dallas Police Department's claim that there was no *"police vehicle in the area of [the rooming house] at about 1:00 p.m."* If the Dallas police actually had contradicted Mrs. Earlene Roberts, which for anyone of goodwill they clearly had not done, it would not make what Earlene Roberts saw and heard untrustworthy. Police cars will often leave their posts with no one at headquarters knowing, some to run personal errands, some to find a hidden place to nap, called "cooping"—short for going to the "chicken coop"—some to commit crimes.

Yet the Dallas Police Department absolutely had not contradicted Earlene Roberts. Chairman Warren's allegation that they had claimed there was no "police vehicle in the area" at 1:00 p.m. simply means that if a Dallas police car was seen "in the area" it would not have been authorized to be there. It would have been there against orders and unlawfully. It would be a beeping police car whose whereabouts were in violation of the Dallas Police Department's accounting of their police vehicles. Being "in the area" against orders and unlawfully appreciably adds to the evidence that this beeping police car was part of a conspiracy, to use Earl Warren's words, to aid *"Oswald in connection with his escape."*

Once Chairman Warren stated that the Dallas Police Department had confirmed there was no "police vehicle in the area," he never again mentioned Earlene Roberts's observations about that patrol car or its active horn. Using his deceitful methodology, Warren simply let that be the end of that issue, dying on the vine. The loyalists and the amateurs reading his report never gave a thought to Earl Warren abruptly dropping Earlene Roberts as a witness like a hot potato, which she was. Earl Warren devoted just one single paragraph (out of 888 pages; see page 163) to Mrs. Earlene Roberts's testimony about Lee Harvey Oswald's pit stop and the beeping police car.

Although Chairman Warren doesn't mention this, Mrs. Earlene Roberts had testified under oath and under penalty of perjury. What Mrs. Roberts saw and heard is not something a person innocently can be mistaken about, like the color of a traffic light. Well then, was she seeing and hearing things? Hallucinating? Was she on speed? Was she insane? Did she have a motive to lie about this?

Any time a prosecution witness with relevant information is doubted by law enforcement, an investigation must take place and a concrete finding must be made that the witness's otherwise-relevant information is either trustworthy or untrustworthy and why. The witness must be interrogated.

I investigated a murder case involving young boys in a wooded area behind a Catholic home for orphans. For loose change the little boys allowed perverts, who sometimes came great distances from other states, to use their penises on the boys' thighs. During one of these encounters a very large and exceedingly strong nine-teen-year-old white man from that Wilmington neighborhood named Meredith Tarbutton attempted to rape a nine-year-old orphaned black boy, Bobby Johnson. Tarbutton had become stim-ulated by pornography at work as a house painter, annoying his coworkers with it. And after work he was now going too far. The rape attempt caused the boy to scream, which caused Tarbutton to stab him to death to shut him up. The little boy still had thirty-five cents, a quarter and a dime that I can still see in the dirt, dropped from his little hand when he was stabbed.

A teenaged male eyewitness, a friend of Tarbutton, claimed that he saw Tarbutton pull the boy into the woods at around 7:30 p.m. Another boy, a preteen who lived nearby and was in his back-yard camping out in a sleeping bag at about 1:30 a.m., heard a boy

140

screaming. The autopsy put the murder in a time range consistent with the 1:30 a.m. screams. This made us suspicious of the teenage boy's claim that he had seen Tarbutton pulling the boy into the woods at 7:30 p.m. It became our job to determine if this teenage witness was trustworthy. Our attorney general's office, unlike most such offices, had its own subpoena power for witnesses. I brought in the teenager who had claimed he saw Tarbutton pulling the victim into the woods at 7:30 p.m. My interrogation revealed that the teenager was lying at Tarbutton's request to throw us off. Tarbutton had an airtight alibi for 7:30 p.m. as he was playing bingo at a Catholic church and had held a lengthy conversation with the priest at 7:30 p.m. Unfortunately, operating under *Miranda*, since Tarbutton had a lawyer, we could ask him no questions about this ploy of his that interrogation of another had just exposed.

No interrogation or cross-examination of Mrs. Earlene Roberts was attempted by Earl Warren. This is a mandatory procedure. It's what professionals automatically do without even thinking about it. Earlene Roberts deserved as much before being dismissed with not even a flimsy excuse. If she were truly untrustworthy, under questioning her testimony would quickly develop huge holes and would fall apart. She'd end up admitting she was confused, lying, or mistaken.

Mrs. Earlene Roberts, however, a retired nurse, was a responsible woman who ran a rooming house and transacted with Oswald for the rental of his room. Two of her five senses were engaged at a time of high alert for the whole nation: sight and sound. She heard the car beeping "several times," saw "a Dallas police car drive slowly by the front of…the premises," saw the car "stopped momentarily," and she heard the car beep again from in front of the rooming house. She saw the car move on, watched it turn at the first corner, and noted that the car's number was not the normal car she was used to seeing. She saw two policemen in the car, not the usual solo officer, and she saw the faces of the two men in the car. She did not recognize either of them, and she knew that neither of the policemen was the normal officer who patrolled that area. Mrs. Roberts saw all this after just learning that the president had been shot, a time when her curiosity would have been heightened.

Had this eyewitness not been kicked off the case, these particular officers would have been findable with her help.

Mrs. Roberts saw Oswald rush past her out the door "hurriedly." Chairman Warren states with approval: *"She has stated that when she last saw Oswald, shortly after 1:00 p.m., he was standing at a bus stop...."*

A bus stop? Oh my, quo vadis, Lee Harvey Oswald?

Standing, not walking or running?

Earl Warren did not give Earlene Roberts a photo display of any officers, not even those who ordinarily used cars with a "0" in the number in second position, much less of every single member of the Dallas Police Department in uniform.

To preserve her evidence, Chairman Warren did not have Mrs. Roberts re-create the events she had seen using a police car and its beeping horn as props so that the events could be filmed, photographed, and everyone would be able to see what she saw from her vantage point forever.

Chairman Warren failed to canvass the neighborhood to determine if any neighbors heard the beeping or saw the police car—not that Mrs. Earlene Roberts needed corroboration. But former District Attorney of Alameda County Earl Warren's failure to order the most basic of police work, a simple door-to-door canvass, demonstrates that for the purposes of his cover-up, the leader of the elevator conspiracy in *Mapp* did not want to risk discovering a corroborating witness who had seen or heard the beeping police car, an incontrovertible symbol of conspiracy that could lead to uncovering a felony murder or two.

Chairman Earl Warren did not take the chance to canvass in order to rule out that a neighbor had a family member or a friend on the force that could have been doing that beeping at 1:00 p.m. Since the beeping was done by the police car and while stopping directly in front of Oswald's rooming house and nowhere else, there is no doubt that the whole neighborhood would have been ruled out as having any connection to a beeping police car, leaving Oswald even more persuasively as the recipient of beeping signals of conspiracy.

Because Mrs. Earlene Roberts saw the car turn at the nearest corner as it drove away, that block and surrounding blocks should have been canvassed as well for any sign of a police car, beeping or not. Due to the assassination, people would have taken notice of police cars in their neighborhoods, as Earlene Roberts had.

Any Dallas security companies whose cars might resemble police cars needed to be ruled out, but they weren't. Again, this most basic of police work would only have served to strengthen Earlene Roberts's eyewitness evidence of Oswald's escape route. All this is something that a former district attorney like Earl Warren would know to do or not do.

Inconsistent with his cold-shoulder treatment of Mrs. Earlene Roberts is that Warren's report relied exclusively on the trustworthiness of her word and ability to observe and report for many other important details. Warren relied on Earlene Roberts for these details because they supported his finding that after Oswald rushed out of the rooming house, he killed Dallas patrol officer J. D. Tippit.

Chairman Warren next wrote these dismissive words: *"Whatever may be the accuracy of Mrs. Roberts's recollection concerning the police car, it is apparent from Mrs. Roberts's further testimony that...."*

Then he relied on Mrs. Roberts for the following evidence:

- Oswald rushed in and out of the rooming house at about 1:00 p.m.;
- Oswald changed some of his clothing;
- Oswald put on a zipper jacket, which could have concealed a handgun;
- Oswald left his rooming house in time to reach on foot Tippit's location at the time Tippit was killed;
- Oswald was on foot and did not enter any vehicle; and

- Oswald was last seen by Earlene Roberts to be standing at the bus stop in front of the rooming house.

The words *"Whatever may be the accuracy of Mrs. Roberts's recollection"* constitute lying by innuendo at its worst. It is far away from a truthful and professional finding that Mrs. Earlene Roberts is an untrustworthy witness or a witness with untrustworthy testimony.

No detective I ever worked with would fail to recognize the enormous value and trustworthiness of this eyewitness regarding these beeping patrolmen in a police car. That is out of place in several ways. Neither of Warren's two hints at a reason to suppress her testimony—namely, her guesses at the cop car number and the Dallas Police Department saying there was no "police car in the area" at 1:00 p.m.—would cause any detective I know to bat an eye for a split second. They are non-reasons for suppressing Earlene Roberts's testimony. They are excuses for a cover-up of the truth of a conspiracy between Lee Harvey Oswald and the two men dressed as Dallas PD patrolmen, all on the road to inadvertently revealing the role of the Mafia in the events of the weekend.

It must be noted that in the single paragraph he devoted to Earlene Roberts, Warren made no judicial ruling that she was incorrect in any way. Nor did he make a judicial ruling that this terrific eyewitness was lying. The chief justice who popularized for the American people the suppression hearing in the *Mapp* conspiracy simply suppressed Mrs. Earlene Roberts's corroborated eyewitness evidence by ignoring it with his "brusque" manner and cold shoulder.

But don't worry, Ike and the rest—Earl Warren's got you covered. He recruited some additional members of the Club. On page 374 of his report, Earl Warren declares with a straight face: *"The conclusion that there is no evidence of a conspiracy was also reached independently by...,"* and then he names seven Kennedy cabinet members and political appointees, such as Secretary of State Dean Rusk, but for purposes of plausible deniability for these cabinet-members-turned-experts-on-conspiracies Warren adds: *"on the basis of the information available to each of them."*

What a shame for the way Mrs. Earlene Roberts was treated. Civilian eyewitnesses in homicide cases need tender loving care. They are more often than not scared to death. No, rather, they are *always* scared to death. And if not cultivated and harvested quickly, some of them lose heart, especially witnesses against police officers, as Mrs. Roberts clearly found herself in a position of being. Mrs. Earlene Roberts died of a stroke two years after giving her testimony. During those two years Dallas officers on patrol would honk their horns when they passed her house. Some fun.

Howard Brennan, an eyewitness who was standing outside the Texas School Book Depository in Dallas, had given the police an accurate description of the man he saw clutching a rifle in the sixth-floor window. It was a description that was used in the police bulletin broadcasts, although he refused to cooperate after Oswald's arrest. He refused to pick Oswald out of a lineup, even though he recognized him as the man in the sixth-floor window with the murder weapon.

When Oswald rushed out of his rooming house, he had neither car nor drivers' license. Lee Harvey Oswald didn't know how to drive a motor vehicle. He couldn't even steal a car. He needed help. He needed wheels. The best and safest means of transportation for a presidential assassin to get to a prearranged destination on that frenzied day in Dallas would have been crouching in the back seat of a police car.

A car horn has but one purpose, and that is to send a signal. It's a means of communication, mostly from one car to another or from a car to a pedestrian, cyclist, or stray dog. But honking a horn is a commonly accepted signal to someone indoors as well. It means "come on out." Although Mrs. Earlene Roberts was expecting no visitors at all on that day, this beeping car was expecting an indoor listener inside this particular house, not a house next door or across the street. It was a signal for Oswald to hurry outside. This was an unusual time, 1:00 p.m., when most people are at work. It was totally inconsistent with his work hours for Lee Harvey Oswald to be there at that time, but he was. And he was able to be there at that exact moment of the honking because Oswald had rushed to get there in a cab and was "all but running" as he entered the rooming house.

That exact house that the two patrolmen drove up to in a marked Dallas police car and stopped in front of at that exact time contained the assassin during the only time he would be there for a momentary pit stop during his escape. And he was there at that time and place to join up with the beeping patrolmen. No homicide investigator I know would listen to Chairman Warren's assertion that the only reason Oswald went there at that time was to change his clothing and pick up his little snub-nosed .38.

Oswald went to the rooming house as a safe location to be picked up by those patrolmen. As a tenant there, his presence at that location would arouse no suspicion.

The Dallas police car's driving slowly up to the house, honking, stopping momentarily in front of the house, honking, and then driving away is evidence that it had been signaling its abandonment of its mission to transport Oswald somewhere. And so he ran out after it.

By virtue of Mrs. Earlene Roberts's testimony that she'd heard the honking at 1:00 p.m. while Oswald was in his room changing clothes, that police car had abandoned its mission as a result of hearing the three bulletin broadcasts of Oswald's general description at 12:45 p.m., 12:48 p.m., and 12:55 p.m. Now that there was a description out there, the two patrolmen's intended passenger was more than simply illegal cargo. "Attention all squads" got these two officers' attention. By 1:00 p.m. Oswald became too hot to transport anywhere. Once the patrolmen heard "Attention all squads" they were beeping good-bye.

After he rushed out, Oswald, indeed, was last seen by Earlene Roberts "standing" at a bus stop in front of the house. All of a sudden he was no longer "all but running." He was "standing." He knew he had missed his ride. If Oswald were seriously looking for the next bus at that stop and it came it would have taken him to the last place on Earth he wanted to go, smack dab back downtown to the vicinity of the crime scene at Dealey Plaza he had just hurried to get away from, that is, in the opposite direction to which he next traveled on foot.

Because of the direction he ultimately traveled the evidence is clear that at that bus stop Lee Harvey Oswald was obviously looking for something other than the next downtown bus. "Standing" at the bus stop is evidence that the shooter, who chose to escape rather than to get caught in the act, was looking for any sign of that unauthorized police car that beeped to him and was now, in his eyes, missing in action. What options did he have? He couldn't be spotted downtown, nor near his address. His only option was to get on foot as far from downtown as possible. He was desperate. If there was a chance in a million that the beeping patrolmen got spooked by something temporarily and were still going to help him, they'd still be in the Oak Cliff area. Oswald likely would have been hopeful that Plan A was still a go. After all, the cops had honked for him. Oswald had heard their signal; they did show up at the rendezvous, so there was still a chance. They wouldn't just leave him out there on the street. Would they? He knew too much. They must know he had gotten stuck in traffic resulting from the assassination.

Oswald would know that the beeping policemen would not look for him at Dealey Plaza, the crime scene, but would look for him in the opposite direction. Oswald did an about-face and headed deeper into his own neighborhood, suburban Oak Cliff. He was now becoming vulnerable to arrest, becoming more like Hinckley than the 007 assassin with an escape plan who had chosen a long-distance target for his rifle, and who had calmly boarded a public bus.

Fifteen minutes after the patrolmen beeped, eyewitnesses saw Oswald less than a mile from his rooming house. He was seen talking to Patrolman J. D. Tippit through the open passenger window of Tippit's patrol car, a two-digit car, number 10, a car with a zero in second position as Earlene's suggested police car numbers had been. Tippit got out of his car and headed toward its front, his gun holstered. Oswald pulled out his .38 and fired across the hood into Tippit's chest.

In 1976 G. Robert Blakey's committee learned that Oswald had started to leave, changed his mind, and walked around the rear of the police car and along its driver's side to the front wheel where Tippit lay shot in the street. Oswald executed Tippit by firing into his right temple. When walking away, Oswald was heard to mutter either, "Poor dumb cop," or "Poor damn cop."

Why did Oswald waste time to hesitate and return to circle around Car 10 and make absolutely sure to silence the officer he had just been speaking to? Obviously, Oswald was afraid he had given away something revealing in his brief conversation with Tippit.

Eyewitnesses followed Oswald to a movie theater where he snuck in without paying, evidence that he was hoping not to have been noticed going in, that he was looking for a Plan B, a place to hide in the dark until he could perhaps locate a pay phone and call his co-conspirator contact to sort things out. However, eyewitnesses to the Tippit murder spoiled his movie theater pit stop by trailing Oswald and calling the police. Oswald was arrested after a scuffle in which he was prevented from shooting one of the officers by that patrolman grabbing Oswald's revolver and preventing him from firing.

On his capture, Oswald exclaimed: *"Well, it's all over now."*

EFW. What was the "it" that was "all over now?" What was going on in Oswald's world that just then suddenly came to be "over"? Chairman Warren didn't ask this question, but the answer was clearly that Plan A, a planned escape, was now "over." What we witnessed, from the last honk of the beeping patrolmen to the last shot fired into Officer Tippit's brain to Lee Harvey Oswald's arrest in a movie theater, is a conspiratorial plan of escape gone haywire.

Earlier, Oswald had departed the bus and grabbed a cab to get to his rooming house. The taxi was at the cabstand of the Greyhound bus terminal, a terminal with buses to faraway places such as Mexico, whose border was capable of being easily penetrated with a visitor's pass. Yet Oswald grabbed a cab instead of a cheap Greyhound bus. He had left his wife, Marina, the bulk of his money, such as it was, when he left for work that morning. He didn't have funds with him for a Greyhound bus. Oswald was clearly sure he wouldn't need getaway money. The only explanation for that is that he expected to be supplied with money by his helpers in Plan A.

Chairman Warren made no attempt at all to even raise the issue of where Oswald was going, much less why he passed up a Greyhound bus. Where he was planning to go was an issue never analyzed or discussed by the veteran homicide prosecutor.

Be that as it may, the only reasonable evidentiary inference any professional investigator could draw from Oswald's passing up a Greyhound for a cab is that Oswald had other plans of escape. A nondriver, he had plans that required help and that included a pit stop at his rooming house. That leads back to the two patrolmen who beeped good-bye, thereby withdrawing their support. This was not an evidentiary trail that Chairman Warren wanted to follow and analyze, and so he ignored it and dismissed Earlene Roberts's testimony.

After leaving $170 in cash and his wedding band behind for his wife, paying cash for his intolerably slow bus ride, and more cash for his cab to hurry him home, Oswald had $13.85 left in his pocket when he was arrested in the movie theater. How far did he expect to get on that? What was a man who chose not to be caught in the first place doing roaming around on foot in the suburban streets with less than twenty dollars for travel money? Without so much as a bag of potato chips to eat? And without grabbing whatever food was available to him at the rooming house, not even an apple. The lack of food provisions is clear proof that Lee Harvey Oswald expected to be fed, likely by his co-conspirators, which means that in his eyes Plan A had two police-officer accomplices with access to food and a safe house.

Merely to ask all these questions totally ignored by Earl Warren heaps on more and more relevant evidence of a conspiracy to help Oswald escape.

By his having so little money in his pocket, there can be no other reasonable inference than that Lee Harvey Oswald expected to be receiving financial aid from the two patrolmen who arrived at his house at the same time he did, were unauthorized to be there, and signaled to him. They are "Patrolman John Doe Number One" and "Patrolman John Doe Number Two," otherwise known as unindicted co-conspirators. Oswald intended to get away but was helpless to do so without their help, and they signaled goodbye.

In the simplest terms, inside that rooming house there was another crime being committed—flight to avoid prosecution—and the beeping patrolmen, unauthorized to be there, passed a signal to the criminal who was inside committing his crime.

CHAPTER THIRTY

A Sample Scenario

For the homicide interrogator, the act of envisioning a scenario is all in a day's work. The interrogator quickly needs to formulate a scenario deduced from the known facts.

Earl Warren's scenario from start to finish was no evidence, no evidence, and no evidence, especially not Earlene Roberts's. Yet at no time did he accuse Earlene Roberts of being an untrustworthy witness as he dismissed her evidence and kept it out of any scenario. Instead, he knew that for purposes of suppressing her evidence the less said about Earlene Roberts, the safer for his real clients, and so Chairman Warren curtailed the topic of Earlene Roberts to a single paragraph. It was a topic, nevertheless, that Warren had no choice but to admit supported the existence of a conspiracy based on Oswald's need of help to escape.

However, once Earlene Roberts and her trustworthy evidence is treated as evidence in a scenario and given the respect it deserves, a much more reasoned scenario of Lee Harvey Oswald's escape plan emerges. Envisioning truthful scenarios in homicide cases is what my colleagues and I did for a living.

What the law and the rules of evidence call reasonable inferences will be made.

What follows will uncover the truth of a conspiracy in Dallas by and among: Carlos Marcello and his New Orleans and Dallas Mafia; Jack Ruby and his lawyer Melvin Belli; Lee Harvey Oswald; and certain members of the Dallas Police Department, in particular Sergeant Patrick Dean.

This professional analytic exercise demonstrating the Dallas conspiracy scenario is this author's attempt at a drawing-room scene in a Mr. Moto or Charlie Chan mystery movie where the investigator assembles the suspects and makes the reasonable inferences and deductions based on the known facts.

CHAPTER THIRTY-ONE

Escape On Foot

Quo vadis, Lee Harvey Oswald? Where were you going on foot? Oak Cliff is a suburb of Dallas. What do they have lots of in suburbs? Houses, houses, and more houses. Suburbs are lousy with houses.

In considering Lee Harvey Oswald's abrupt leaving of that corner bus stop, doing an about face, and trudging deeper on foot into the suburb of Oak Cliff, a reasonable inference would be that Oswald had been led to believe by whoever was using him as a "lone disposable nut" that the honking police car was going to pick him up near the bus stop at his rooming house. In his changed clothes, and now wearing a jacket, Oswald was going to be driven to what he was told would be a safe house in the Oak Cliff suburbs where he could lie low until the heat died down, and then he would be transported by private plane to a safe destination with a bulge of money in his pocket to give to his wife. In reality, this suburban house would be an unsafe house where the "lone cowboy" Oswald would be disposed of, the way Jimmy Hoffa was. Of course, such a phony safe house could not have been shown to Oswald in advance because he might then reveal its location to a third party. Since he didn't drive, Oswald would need to have been escorted to the house after the assassination.

In this part of the conspiracy scenario, and to anyone who understands how Mafia bosses think, when Jack Ruby's police felt the heat they beeped goodbye, bailed out, and abandoned their mission as transporters of Lee Harvey Oswald to his death and disappearance. His Mafia bosses held Jack Ruby responsible for his policemen's actions. It now became Jack Ruby's responsibility to atone for his officers having abandoned their chauffeuring job. Under Mafia protocol, and considering the access Jack Ruby had to the Dallas Police Department, it became Ruby's responsibility to complete the silencing of Oswald before Oswald became worn down by the virtually unlimited interrogation of that era.

Interestingly, this scenario is what our life's experiences had led my mother, sister, and me to believe from the time we saw Oswald's interrogation interrupted by Jack Ruby on live television, an unshaken belief solidly confirmed by my research for this book.

Further, in considering Lee Harvey Oswald and his actions in suburban Oak Cliff, it is clear that Oswald had aroused Officer J. D. Tippit's interest because Oswald was taking an unusual interest in Tippit's Dallas Police Department car, number 10, while in the process of searching for his assigned patrolmen in a car with a number with a zero in the second position, a number like 10.

It's a reasonable inference that Oswald shot Officer Tippit in the chest to prevent getting himself arrested for carrying a concealed deadly weapon, and in the course of that arrest, being exposed as the Kennedy assassin. After shooting Tippit in the chest with a relatively loud gun, Oswald headed away. It was his job to flee, to run. But then, as we learned from the overlooked witness discovered by G. Robert Blakey's team, Jack Ray Tatum, Lee Harvey Oswald hesitated, changed his direction, and returned to finish off Tippit in the temple for yet a different reason. Oswald had already secured his getaway by shooting Tippit in the chest. Why did he take the time to draw further attention to himself by returning to the scene of that crime and firing yet another shot, administering a coup de grâce? As part of this conspiracy scenario, the best, reasonable inference that could explain this strange return and execution is that through the open passenger window Oswald had said something about his missing patrolmen's car that had sparked Officer Tippit's curiosity enough to cause him to get out of his car and walk into his death. Perhaps it was something like: "I'm looking for a cop car that's patrolling Oak Cliff. Is there another Dallas cop car around here with two cops?"

That is the most likely reasonable explanation for why Oswald slowed his getaway on foot enough to walk back to fire another loud shot and execute Tippit in the right temple, silencing him forever.

By asking about another prowling patrol car, Oswald would have revealed to Tippit too much about his quo vadis conspiracy to escape to allow Tippit to live. Oswald had to be concerned that Tippit might survive long enough to radio that his killer was looking for a Dallas police car with two officers in it, thereby destroying what extremely thin chance Oswald had to revive his escape plan by finding the two patrolmen. And that explains why Officer Tippit was a "poor, dumb cop" in Oswald's eyes. It also explains why Oswald did not bother to steal Tippit's loaded gun still in his holster or steal any cash on Tippit's person. Oswald's only interest was in silencing Tippit.

The standard loyalist and conspiracy speculation that Officer Tippit had spotted Oswald, had become suspicious of him in connection with the assassination, had exchanged a few words with him through the open passenger window, and had gotten out of his police car to confront him when Oswald suddenly opened fire at Tippit's chest totally fails to explain Oswald's U-turn back to ensure the silencing of Tippit.

To the contrary, Officer Tippit could not have suspected Oswald, far from downtown and walking leisurely in Oak Cliff, of being the presidential assassin because Officer Tippit never drew his gun. It was in his holster when he died. It's as simple as that, except for those writers inexperienced with police procedures or who deep down don't think police are professionals. Conspiracy authors, fostering their theories, read into this holstered gun all kinds of nonsense linking Oswald to Tippit as prior acquaintances if not co-conspirators. Professional investigators know that the only significance to Officer Tippit not drawing his gun is that he did not suspect Oswald was dangerous. There is no patrolman anywhere who confronts any potential murder suspect with his gun in his holster, much less a potential murder suspect in a presidential assassination.

More to the point, Tippit never ordered Oswald to put up his hands.

Further, the assassination of the president had taken place in another part of town. It had taken place relatively recently, about a half hour prior, and this young man was on foot.

G. Robert Blakey and Gary Cornwell, and by extension their whole staff of forty-five investigators and experts on the House Select Committee on Assassinations, which had discovered the new witness Jack Ray Tatum, did not offer any other reasonable inference as to why Lee Harvey Oswald had fired that final fatal shot finishing off Officer Tippit.

My deduced scenario of Oswald's cold-blooded silencing of Officer Tippit springs from and is based on Earlene Roberts's trustworthy eyewitness testimony that she had seen two "beeping" Dallas patrolmen come and go while her tenant, Lee Harvey Oswald, was changing some of his clothing as a disguise and was grabbing the revolver he used a few minutes later to slaughter a "poor, dumb" cop just doing his job. The beeping patrolmen evidence, once included in the case, leads to the reasonable inference that Oswald was looking for two patrolmen in a patrol car while desperately roaming Oak Cliff on foot.

On his arrest in the movie theater Oswald had in his wallet a curious document. It was a counterfeit Selective Service card, commonly called a draft card. This one was in the name of "Alek James Hidell," the same name Oswald used as his alias when he bought his guns in March 1963 in an era when no identification was needed to buy a gun.

Dallas Police detective Gus Rose processed Oswald for Tippit's murder on arrival at the Dallas Police Department's third-floor Detective Division. Detective Rose stated in his report:

> *I took the man to an interrogation office. I removed his handcuffs. I asked him to identify himself. He refused.*
>
> *In his pockets I found pieces of identification. One card was for Lee Harvey Oswald; the other was for Alek Hidell.*
>
> *"Which are you?"*
>
> *"You're the cop. You figure it out."*
>
> *He told me a lot of lies. Captain Fritz called me out at some time near 2:20 p.m. He said that the employees of the Texas School Book Depository were accounted for; except one. He told me to get some men together and get out to this address in Irving. I asked what the man's name was. He said, "Lee Harvey Oswald." I was stunned. "Captain," I said. "I think this is Oswald, right in there."*

By Oswald's tough-guy reaction to the Alek Hidell identification issue, Oswald is revealing that this was a hot-button issue for him. He refused to answer any questions about it that day or the next, even after conceding his own real identity. During Sunday morning's interrogation, just before Ruby's gut-shot of Oswald, the homicide chief, Captain Will Fritz, again asked Oswald about the Alek Hidell identification. Even though he had yet to say a word about it, according to the interrogation report: *"Oswald became angry and said, 'Now I've told you all I'm going to tell you about that card in my billfold—you have the card yourself and you know as much about it as I do.'"*

The Selective Service draft card ID in the name of Alek Hidell was useless in America. Young men over eighteen all had draft cards and were required to carry them at all times. And like almost all ID in that era, such as drivers' licenses, draft cards had no photo on them. Strangely, this one did, a photo of Oswald beneath the false name "Alek Hidell."

Oswald also carried in his wallet a counterfeit Marine Service card in the name of Alek James Hidell. Neither piece of false ID had been found during the police inventory of Oswald's wallet when he was arrested in a fistfight with anti-Castro Cuban exiles on August 9, 1963, in New Orleans three months prior. This gives rise to the inference that Oswald created the false identification subsequent to that August 9 arrest and before this November 22 arrest.

While Chairman Warren's report acknowledged both the counterfeit draft card's existence and the Marine Service card, Chairman Warren made no attempt to understand Oswald's possible use of this laughably fake ID. Nor does any book on "Dallas" that I consulted, and I feel as if I have consulted almost all. There it is and there it remains, according to one and all, a passing fact of no consequence, just two pieces of *fugazi* ID unusable in America and with one piece having Oswald's photo on it for some ignored reason. It all got the cold shoulder by Earl Warren.

But "attention all squads," it is ID usable in certain poorly developed places outside America's border where they're not familiar with American draft cards: places to which Oswald would think he needed to be flown.

Oswald's mere possession of escape ID usable in a foreign country when he had $13.85 in his pocket with which to travel or use once in a foreign country is further corroboration of the beeping patrolmen conspiracy. It is trustworthy and relevant evidence that Oswald expected help, more proof of a conspiracy between Oswald and the beeping patrolmen, but not yet tied to Jack Ruby.

CHAPTER THIRTY-TWO

Pinocchio

After gut-shooting and snuffing out the life of Oswald, silencing him forever, Jack Ruby, not yet possessing a *Miranda* mute button for lawyering up, had no choice but to answer questions. He told the authorities numerous obvious falsehoods regarding what he was doing and where he was doing it in the nearly two days between President Kennedy's last breath and Oswald's last breath.

Jack Ruby's serial telltale lies constitute the second giant neon key to unlocking a Mafia conspiracy, this time in permanent black ink tying Oswald and the beeping patrolmen to Jack Ruby in a conspiracy to kill President Kennedy.

At 2:00 p.m., an hour and a half after slaying President Kennedy, and now as a cop killer, the "nut" Oswald landed in hefty Captain Will Fritz's homicide squad room in the Dallas Police Department. Protocol required that Oswald be transferred from the Dallas PD jail to the sheriff's jail, a quick nine blocks away. But it was convenient for the Dallas homicide interrogators to keep Oswald at the Dallas PD jail for a day or so. Transfer to the sheriff's custody could wait.

The homicide squad was in Room 317 on the third floor of the Dallas Police Department. Except for sleeping in a jail cell on the fifth floor at night, Oswald was kept in the homicide squad room from the time he arrived on Friday at 2:00 p.m. until Ruby gut-shot him in the Dallas PD basement on Sunday morning at 11:21.

Oswald was interrogated repeatedly in approximately twelve sessions in less than two days that were fit in between other official procedures.

Dallas police chief Jesse Curry on Friday, allegedly to curry favor with the press, permitted a media circus in the third-floor hallway outside the door to homicide. Every time Oswald was moved from that room to the elevator for a trip to the basement to attend the three lineups or the two arraignments for killing President Kennedy and Officer Tippit, he was bombarded by questions from the press, which was literally in his face, all but hugging him, nose-to-nose.

As the gifted interrogator and chief of homicide, Captain Will Fritz, expressed it, the crowd on Friday *forced us to move this prisoner through hundreds of people each time he was carried from my office to the jail door, some twenty feet...."*

This was the "parading" of Oswald I had objected to while the eggplant cooked at my mother's house.

The hallway was so crowded that the Dallas district attorney Henry Wade said: *"You just had to fight your way down through the hall, through the press...."*

(Incidentally, ten years later in 1973, Henry Wade, a close friend and Texas political ally of President Johnson, was on the losing side of the Supreme Court's 1973 abortion case of *Roe v. Wade*.)

For those many observers who question why Jack Ruby didn't shoot Oswald in the third-floor hallway during one of the many transfers of Oswald through "the hundreds of people," it's worth quoting the evidence-destroying FBI agent James P. Hosty, Jr., in his book *Assignment: Oswald* (Arcade Publishing, 1996): *"As I stepped through the [third-floor] stairwell door, I was overwhelmed by the sights and sounds.... The place was in an uproar; people had to shout into each other's ears to be heard."*

A young local Dallas CBS reporter, Dan Rather, used the phrase "a tsunami of reporters" to describe that hallway on Friday.

Besides, although the incident was given the Warren "cold shoulder," Ruby did try to kill Oswald on the third floor a little later on Friday, as witnessed by reporter Victor Robertson.

On Thursday night, twenty-four hours before this "tsunami" and the night before the assassination of President Kennedy, strip club owner and Oswald shooter Jack Ruby had a relaxed dinner in Dallas at the Egyptian Lounge. The Egyptian Lounge was owned by Joe Campisi, the Dallas Mafia underboss to Joe Civello, who was the Mafia boss for Carlos Marcello of New Orleans and Dallas. It was a restaurant that after closing hours became an illegal gambling casino.

After dinner, Jack Ruby went to the bar at the Dallas Cabana Hotel, built with a $3.6-million loan from Jimmy Hoffa's Central States Pension Fund of the Teamsters Union.

Three days after Ruby silenced Oswald—interrogation interrupted—mob-connected lawyer Melvin Belli of San Francisco quickly showed up at the Cabana to set up shop as Ruby's lawyer.

Jack Ruby had an alibi for the time of the assassination, 12:30 p.m. on Friday. As was his custom on Fridays at that time, Ruby was at the newspaper working on ads for his two strip clubs. According to an employee witness, he remained there "sitting at the same spot... reading a newspaper" after he finished the ads. This act established his alibi and put Ruby in a position to get the latest news on the success of the assassination.

Another "employee entered the office and announced that shots had been fired at the president" and that Kennedy was at Parkland Hospital, condition unknown. Ruby stopped reading his newspaper and drove to Parkland Hospital.

National reporter Seth Kantor had flown to Dallas from Washington, DC, as part of the president's press party, and knew Jack Ruby from his reporting days in Dallas. To get Kantor's attention, although it was denied by Ruby, he tugged on Kantor's jacket at Parkland Hospital "inside the main entrance."

Wilma May Tice, a former Dallas city employee, was at Parkland at the same time. She testified that she had heard a man be addressed by the name "Jack." Later, she saw Ruby's picture in the newspaper and positively identified Ruby as the "Jack" she had seen at Parkland. Seth Kantor testified that *"Ruby called me by my first name."*

Ruby asked Seth if he thought Ruby should close his two night-clubs for three days, which Ruby ultimately did do. Seth Kantor was called away from Ruby by the 1:30 p.m. press conference announcing that President Kennedy had died at 1:00 p.m.

The president's time of death was the same time the beeping patrolmen had signaled good-bye to Oswald at 1:00 p.m. on Friday.

Forty-six hours after talking to Seth Kantor at Parkland, Ruby shot and killed Oswald in the basement of the Dallas Police Department in front of seventy armed policemen guarding Oswald's transfer to a car that was to transport Oswald from the police department jail to the nearby sheriff's jail.

On questioning in custody, Jack Ruby looked every one of his interrogators in their eyes and brazenly denied ever going to Parkland Hospital, much less encountering Seth Kantor there.

Why would Ruby lie about having been at Parkland, having seen Kantor there, and having talked to Kantor there?

Ruby's lies denying that he went to Parkland Hospital and had a conversation with Seth Kantor, like any and all lies told by a suspect in a crime, are independent evidence of guilt and guilty knowledge. It's the equivalent of a confession. His particular lies give rise to a reasonable inference that Ruby went to Parkland in the role of a conspirator anxious to check on the president's medical condition and to report back to his co-conspirator bosses. Because Ruby knew he was at Parkland Hospital in his role as a conspirator, checking on things for his bosses, he denied ever being there. Lies are evidence of guilt, and there was no other reason to lie about his otherwise-innocent trip to Parkland or his equally innocent encounter with Seth Kantor.

Just as brazenly as Ruby lied, Chairman Earl Warren chose to aid and abet Ruby in his lies. Earl Warren chose to suppress Seth Kantor's testimony because Ruby's act of going to Parkland Hospital for medical news would be an important piece of relevant evidence that the man who two days later shot and silenced Lee Harvey Oswald was a conspirator in President Kennedy's killing.

And so, as he did with Earlene Roberts, again without using the word "untrustworthy," which would have been impossible to apply to a reporter of Seth Kantor's stature, Earl Warren found Seth Kantor's word to be untrustworthy and no match for *Ruby's* word.

Essentially, Chairman Warren accused Seth Kantor of not being able to tell time. With no evidence but Mafia associate Jack Ruby's word, Warren claimed in his report that Seth Kantor actually saw Jack Ruby not at Parkland at 1:30 p.m. in the afternoon, where Wilma Tice had also seen Ruby, but ten hours later that night at the Dallas police station during a midnight basement press conference. This midnight basement press conference was at a time and place in which Jack Ruby was standing up on a table above the crowd and was photographed in the background of a news photographer's picture, plain as day. It was at a time and place Jack Ruby admitted to being, even though he'd had no business being there. I submit that it was due to the existence of the photograph that Ruby freely admitted to being there at the midnight basement press conference.

However, Seth Kantor remained steadfast. As a reporter, he was trained and experienced in reporting his observations. He knew the difference between night and day and the difference between "the main entrance" of a hospital and the basement of a crowded police station.

Chairman Earl Warren suborned Jack Ruby's perjury about Parkland Hospital and Seth Kantor because Warren was on the same side of these murders as was Jack Ruby.

Earl Warren let us know in no uncertain terms in his report: *"Ruby has firmly denied going to Parkland."* And that's all there is to that, folks.

As with the eyewitness Earlene Roberts who'd had her curiosity aroused by the calculated actions of the two patrolmen, this was a memorable encounter at Parkland Hospital. Seth Kantor and Jack Ruby spoke meaningful English words to each other. Jack Ruby tugged at Seth Kantor's jacket to get his attention and called him "Seth." They knew each other. I can't imagine the most incompetent law enforcement officer in history siding with Jack Ruby's lies on this.

Of course, I think it's fair to say we know by now that when we're dealing with Earl Warren, we're not dealing with incompetence.

Ruby's first two tall tales were set straight many years following Ruby's 1967 death from lung cancer. G. Robert Blakey's committee in 1979 took a vote and sided with Seth Kantor, declaring Jack Ruby to have been lying about not going to Parkland and about not seeing and talking to Seth Kantor while there.

In 1963 Leon Hubert was a Warren Commission staff lawyer, a worker bee in charge of investigating Jack Ruby. He believed the Warren Commission was purposefully ignoring the important subject of Jack Ruby's ties to organized crime and ignoring the investigation into Jack Ruby generally. Exasperated, Leon Hubert quit the commission. But first he had established several lies Jack Ruby had told during interrogation, which grossly minimized the number of Ruby's trips to Cuba. While these Cuba lies are significant in demonstrating Jack Ruby's connections to the Mafia and to his securing Florida boss Santo Trafficante's release from Castro's jail, the lies Jack Ruby told about not being at Parkland on Friday, not speaking with Seth Kantor there, and his subsequent lies about not being at other relevant locations on Friday and on Saturday are key lies that add to the proof that Jack Ruby was a co-conspirator with Lee Harvey Oswald in the assassination of President Kennedy.

It's not that the lies merely degrade Jack Ruby's credibility, like the lies about his trips to Cuba, which they do. It's that the act of lying itself, like flight from the scene of a crime, is independent evidence of his guilt on the relevant topic of his lies. These were lies to cover up a conspiracy to silence Lee Harvey Oswald. These were telltale lies, at least three right out of the gate:

1. Ruby said he didn't go to Parkland.
2. Ruby said he didn't have a conversation with Seth Kantor at Parkland.
3. Ruby denied tugging on Seth Kantor's jacket at Parkland.

As the evidence mounts it will be seen that these were lies to cover up a Mafia conspiracy to use the "nut" Lee Harvey Oswald to shoot President Kennedy, and then to use Ruby to shoot Oswald.

On the day of the assassination, in the early evening around 7:00, with Oswald in custody and the subject of ongoing interrogation, five separate eyewitnesses plainly saw Jack Ruby in the third-floor Dallas Police Department hallway outside Captain Fritz's homicide squad room 317. Four of the five eyewitnesses knew Jack Ruby personally.

A day later, during Ruby's interrogation after killing Oswald, just as he had claimed that he had never gone to Parkland Hospital and spoken to Seth Kantor, Ruby brazenly claimed he wasn't at the Dallas Police Department on Friday in the early evening. Jack Ruby claimed he first set foot in the Dallas Police Department building on Friday sometime after 11:15 p.m., shortly before the midnight press conference held in the basement conference room where Oswald was exhibited to the press to demonstrate that he was not being roughed up, and where Ruby was photographed standing on a table in the background.

Once again Chairman Warren chose to aid and abet, to support and cover for Jack Ruby. In his report, Chairman Warren concluded that these five eyewitnesses who had seen Ruby on a relatively orderly third floor at 7:00 p.m. couldn't tell time. And they couldn't tell the difference between the third-floor hallway outside the squad room and the basement conference room. Earl Warren, using his brazen methodology, decided that these five eyewitnesses, indeed, saw Jack Ruby but they saw him five hours later than each testified they had seen him. Chairman Warren wrote in his report that the five eyewitnesses had not seen Jack Ruby on the third floor outside the homicide squad room at 7:00 p.m., a significant time and place for Ruby, but that all five had seen Ruby in the Dallas PD basement conference room around midnight.

Chairman Warren lumped these five eyewitnesses with Seth Kantor and threw the gang of six eyewitnesses into the basement conference room at midnight. In doing so, Warren pinned the false badge of truth-teller on Ruby and suppressed the clear evidence that by repeated lying Ruby had virtually signed a series of confessions.

The first of the five eyewitnesses, A. M. Eberhardt, a vice squad detective who knew Ruby well, testified under oath that he saw Ruby on the third floor between 6:00 and 7:00 Friday evening. Eberhardt shook Ruby's hand, held a conversation with Ruby, and testified that Ruby talked about how bad the "assassination was for the city of Dallas." Eberhardt said, "...*Ruby carried a note pad and professed to be a translator for the Israeli press,*" and that Rudy called Oswald a "zero." Considering that vice is the squad that would have the most professional contact with the owner of two clip joints, one would think this eyewitness, a trained observer, was unassailable. Now, how was Earl Warren going to get around this eyewitness? He was going to have some struggle with what Jack Ruby was doing outside the homicide squad room at a time when Oswald was the subject of interrogation. More importantly, he was going to have to struggle with why, once again, Ruby had lied in detail about it.

On examination of each, I submit there was a very obvious reason for Chairman Warren to suppress the evidence offered by all five of these 7:00 p.m. eyewitnesses.

Next, John Rutledge was a reporter for the *Dallas Morning News*, the same newspaper in which Jack Ruby ran his regular ads and in which office Jack Ruby read the newspaper during the assassination, his alibi. John Rutledge testified that he saw Jack Ruby either at 6:00 or 7:00 on the third floor on Friday evening. John Rutledge knew "Jack" very well. Chairman Warren's report quotes John Rutledge:

> I saw Jack and two out-of-state reporters, whom I did not know,
> leave the elevator door and proceed toward those television cameras,

to go around the corner where Captain Fritz's office was. Jack walked between them. These two out-of-state reporters had big press cards pinned on their coats, great big red ones, I think they said "President Kennedy's Visit to Dallas—Press," or something like that. And Jack didn't have one, but the man on either side of him did. And they walked pretty rapidly from the elevator area past the policeman, and Jack was bent over like this—writing on a piece of paper and talking to one of the reporters and pointing to something on the piece of paper, he was kind of hunched over.

With remarkably detailed observations, Rutledge fully corroborated Detective A. M. Eberhardt. John Rutledge had seen Jack Ruby fraudulently posing as a newsman's helper at the same time Detective Eberhardt saw Jack Ruby fraudulently posing as a newsman's helper. John Rutledge described actions that only could have occurred on the third floor and could not have occurred in the basement: "the elevator door," "the television cameras," and "Captain Fritz's office."

There were three more equally credible eyewitnesses who saw Jack Ruby on the third floor around 7:00 Friday evening. They were another Dallas PD detective named Roy Standifer; a KBOX news editor named Ronald Lee Jenkins; and a Dallas reporter, the key eyewitness of the five, Victor Robertson of WFAA. Victor Robertson is the eyewitness whose testimony proves the existence of a preexisting conspiracy between Jack Ruby and Lee Harvey Oswald. As Earlene Roberts would have been the star witness for any honest homicide investigator, Victor Robertson would have been a close second. From Roberts to Robertson for the double play to unlocking the secrets of Dallas.

Jack Ruby denied going to the Dallas Police Department building until closer to the midnight hour because he knew he had done something dangerous at 7:00 p.m. there that would prove he was stalking Oswald, and a 7:00 p.m. attempt on Oswald's life by Ruby proves that forever. If only Chairman Warren had not been feeding us Ruby's lies we would not have had to endure decades of suppressed truth.

Motive is not an element that it is essential to prove in a murder case. But Jack Ruby's motive to silence Lee Harvey Oswald is the easy way to prove that a conspiracy existed between the two men. If Jack Ruby had shot Oswald with the motive to silence Oswald, that means that Oswald possessed conspiratorial information that needed to be suppressed. Proving Ruby's motive was to silence Oswald also proves that Jack Ruby knew Lee Harvey Oswald's memory bank contained evidence of a preexisting conspiracy between the two men. It proves that Jack Ruby feared that under effective interrogation, Oswald could implicate Ruby in the assassination itself or in Oswald's escape, which amounts to the same thing. Proving that Jack Ruby's motive was to silence Oswald proves the existence and nature of that conspiracy.

In the law of evidence, it is a fair and reasonable inference that the man who shot Oswald on Sunday morning was looking for an opportunity to shoot him on Friday around 7:00 p.m., trying to gain access to him by posing as a newsman's helper. Ruby later admitted that he had his snub-nosed .38 in his right front trouser pocket at the Friday midnight press conference, and in light of his lies regarding his 7:00 p.m. whereabouts, this allows an inference that he had it in his pocket five hours earlier as well. Ruby was known to carry his gun all the time.

The stalking of Oswald on Friday around 7:00 p.m. with the intent to shoot him isn't, in and of itself, evidence of the motive to silence Oswald. Jack Ruby might have had a different motive to shoot Oswald. He might have been overcome with grief and enraged at Oswald. Ruby might have been a "nut," a "lone cowboy."

That's why a motive to silence cannot be assumed from Ruby's shooting of Oswald. It requires additional evidence, however slight. What could provide evidence is that Oswald was being interrogated every day when he was shot, and he would be interrogated under more favorable conditions for his interrogators once he was transferred to the relative peace and quiet of the sheriff's jail. That Oswald was being interrogated repeatedly was common knowledge, and the status of the interrogations was fed to the press daily by Chief Curry. Oswald was interrogated the very morning he was shot.

However, in murder, common knowledge cannot be attributed to a suspect. Actual knowledge by Jack Ruby that Lee Harvey Oswald was being interrogated at the time of the jailhouse murder is the most persuasive evidence.

This analysis of the law of conspiracy is something that Chief Justice Warren certainly knew.

Evidence that Jack Ruby had actual knowledge that Oswald was being interrogated came from the WFAA reporter, Victor Robertson. This made Victor Robertson nearly as big a problem for Chairman Warren as Mrs. Earlene Roberts.

Victor Robertson, like all the other eyewitnesses, was a trained observer, and like Seth Kantor he knew Jack Ruby personally. Victor Robertson had "no doubts" about what he both saw and heard and the time and place he saw and heard it.

On the third floor of the Dallas PD around 7:00 p.m. Victor Robertson saw Jack Ruby approach the Room 317 office door that had a glass panel in the upper half of the door. The glass-paneled door opened in from the hallway and led to a small outer office with a built-in closet on the left and Captain Fritz's glass-walled office on the right. Not glass blocks, but plain glass with its occupants clearly visible through the glass panel on the door.

Once inside Room 317, it is a stride into Captain Fritz's office, where Oswald was being interrogated.

The glass panel in the door is a crucial detail in proving the existence of a conspiracy, but Chairman Warren omitted any mention of the glass panel in the door in his report. That Captain Fritz's office was glass walled is an even more important detail in proving the existence of a conspiracy, but Earl Warren omitted this from his report, as well.

In his book *Assignment: Oswald*, FBI special agent James P. Hosty, Jr., a felonious flusher of evidence, described standing in the homicide squad room's little outer office and being able to see both the third-floor hallway through the glass-paneled door and, with a slight turn of his head, the occupants, including Lee Harvey Oswald, in Captain Fritz's glass-walled office:

> *Having finished my transcribing, I…walked back into the outer office. In the hallway the press was still in a frenzy. Rubbing the back of my neck, I glanced over and looked through the glass wall to Fritz's office. I watched as a phone was placed in front of Oswald and watched as Oswald placed a call. I couldn't hear him, but I could see Oswald calmly speaking into the mouthpiece, occasionally pausing to listen. After a few minutes he hung up and leaned back in his chair.*

This, presumably, was at some time other than the time of Victor Robertson's observations. Hosty's observations are recorded here merely to describe the scene and what could be seen through the glass by Ruby.

At 7:00 p.m. Friday, from the hallway, Victor Robertson saw Jack Ruby put his hand on the Room 317 doorknob, turn it, and start to move into the homicide squad office, which had Jack Ruby gained entrance would have brought him within a stride of the interrogation of Lee Harvey Oswald going on in Captain Will Fritz's room.

Victor Robertson said about Jack Ruby: *"He had the door open a few inches and began to step into the room."*

Further, Victor Robertson said that Jack Ruby was stopped from getting any closer to the interrogation of Oswald. One of two police officers guarding the office door said, *"You can't go in there, Jack."*

Victor Robertson heard that and saw "Jack" back away and retreat down the third-floor hallway toward the elevator.

As Chairman Warren was forced to admit in his report, Victor Robertson said he saw Ruby "unsuccessfully attempt to enter the Homicide office."

The reasonable inference regarding the man who shot Oswald is that Jack Ruby unsuccessfully tried to get in to the interrogation in progress to shoot Oswald.

Jack Ruby's attempt to get in past a closed and guarded door carries with it the further reasonable inference that Ruby was purposefully attempting to barge into the interrogation within. Ruby plainly could see through the glass panel while standing at the doorway before putting his hand on the doorknob. As the man who would kill Oswald, Jack Ruby's goal was the killing and silencing of Oswald at that moment. Before "Jack" was stopped by the policeman, once inside the outer office all Jack Ruby had to do was take a good crouching step and reach out for the doorknob to Captain Fritz's office, push the door in, and get one or more shots off in a relatively peaceful setting in front of unsuspecting policemen and away from the raucous "tsunami" of the third-floor hallway.

Jack Ruby, standing in front of the glass-paneled door of homicide, easily saw Lee Harvey Oswald being interrogated.

Victor Robertson provided the proof that Jack Ruby knew of the interrogation. He'd seen it. And then Ruby brazenly tried to get into it to shoot Oswald. Victor Robertson provided the evidence that what Jack Ruby did on Sunday morning, he had tried to do in the early evening on Friday around 7:00.

Ruby lied about even being in the building, adding to his guilt.

It had been a busy day. This was the day President Kennedy was assassinated at 12:30 p.m., both Oswald and the beeping patrolmen arrived at the rooming house at 1:00 p.m., Officer Tippit was executed at 1:15 p.m., and both Ruby and journalist Seth Kantor arrived at Parkland Hospital just prior to a 1:30 p.m. hospital press conference to announce the president's death. At 2:00 p.m. Oswald was arrested in a movie theater for Officer Tippit's murder; at 3:00 p.m. Oswald was arrested for the assassination of President Kennedy. By 7:00 p.m. Jack Ruby was on a mission to kill Oswald, and Victor Roberson saw him at work.

Jack Ruby made the evidence for a conspiracy incontrovertible by his telltale lies about the early evening around 7:00, denying that he was ever in the Dallas Police Department building until the midnight basement press conference.

Jack Ruby's motive to silence Oswald, to prevent the further interrogation of Oswald by shooting him, is supplied by Victor Robertson, and a conspiracy is proven. It is proven by Jack Ruby's behavior at the door of the homicide office, behavior demonstrating his eyewitness knowledge that he knew Oswald had been the subject of interrogation when Ruby shot and killed him. With proof of Ruby's motive to silence Oswald, the preexisting conspiracy between Oswald and Ruby is solidly established.

Because of the power of Victor Robertson's evidence, and because of the mandate from President Johnson and Robert F. Kennedy, Earl Warren had to treat Victor Robertson worse than he had treated Mrs. Earlene Roberts.

Chairman Earl Warren chose to claim in his report that what Victor Robertson saw and heard didn't happen because Jack Ruby wasn't at the police station at 7:00 p.m., the time claimed by Robertson and the other four credible eyewitnesses.

To further help Ruby's lies, Earl Warren argued in his report that policemen "on duty near Homicide" didn't remember "the episode."

The memory lapse of an undisclosed number of policemen in the hallway and doorway does not make untrustworthy the very trustworthy Victor Robertson, who plainly said Ruby "unsuccessfully attempted to enter the Homicide office." As with Mrs. Roberts, Mr. Robertson saw and heard a complete incident, an eyebrow raiser of an incident, from start to finish a memorable encounter.

For patrolmen in the hall to remember "the episode" would have required the patrolmen guarding Oswald to admit to their failure to investigate. Why would any civilian ever open a door to gain access to an interrogation room during an interrogation in progress? Much less during the interrogation of the suspect in two murder cases, the killer of a policeman, during the interrogation of the assassin of President Kennedy? Competent patrolmen guarding Oswald at that door, at the very least, were required to find out why "Jack" was trying to barge in there. At a minimum they needed to eject him from the building permanently.

Any patrolman with sense who was questioned after Jack Ruby shot Oswald instinctively would say: "If anyone attempted to breach the integrity of an interrogation in progress, I certainly would have looked into it."

These police officers would have been honest policemen in self-protection mode.

Earl Warren next contradicted himself without realizing it when he wrote that there actually was one police officer who had "remembered the episode," but this police officer "remembered" that it wasn't Jack Ruby who tried to get into Room 317.

Okay, so "the episode" *did* happen as Victor Robertson said, but with an anonymous intruder, not Jack Ruby. Therefore, the two policemen "on duty near Homicide" at 7:00 p.m. who didn't remember the incident are wrong and irrelevant because the incident happened according to the officer who "remembered the episode." Those two policemen who didn't "remember the episode" are the fluffy parts of a half-baked attempt by Chairman Warren to suppress Victor Robertson's testimony.

As for the policeman who "remembered the episode," Earl Warren didn't attempt to have him explain another policeman's use of the name "Jack," as in, *You can't go in there, Jack."* Warren made no attempt to so much as mention this inconsistency. I don't know a detective who would fail to ask a ton of follow-up questions of the policeman who thought "Jack" wasn't Jack Ruby. And at the end of the ton of questioning, any professional investigator would take Victor Robertson's version over anyone else's.

None of these police officers helping the shameless Earl Warren succeeded in making Victor Robertson untrustworthy, and so Warren tried another desperate gambit and wrote that Victor Robertson viewed Ruby "from the rear." With Ruby trying to surge his way into the squad room, of course he'd be viewed "from the rear." Ruby's looks and body frame are distinctive.

Again, Victor Robertson was positive that it was his friend Jack Ruby who had tried to gain entrance into the ongoing interrogation in Captain Fritz's office. Victor Robertson said he had "no doubts." He heard Jack Ruby called "Jack," and respond to the name "Jack" by beating a hasty retreat.

Both Victor Robertson and this latest officer who "remembered the episode" but thought it wasn't Jack Ruby were shown the same photo display by the FBI. Robertson identified Ruby "without any qualification." The officer, on the other hand, admitted that *"he did not feel that he knew Ruby well enough to make an unqualified identification."*

Not that Victor Robertson needed corroboration, but John Rutledge, the reporter for *the Dallas Morning News* who corroborated Detective Eberhardt about Jack Ruby posing as a newsman's helper, reported that he had seen Jack Ruby at about 7:00 p.m. outside the homicide squad door behind which Oswald was being interrogated in plain view through plain glass. Jack Ruby knew just where to station himself.

As an aside, for safety reasons, interrogators almost always leave their guns outside the door of an interrogation room. Had Jack Ruby gotten into Fritz's office with his gun, likely he'd have found a roomful of unarmed police.

If Ruby was willing to admit he was at the Dallas PD after 11:15 Friday night, what possible harm is there in admitting he was there five hours sooner, around 7:00? The only harm is that was the time he knew he brazenly tried to elbow his way into the interrogation room to kill Oswald. Ruby's falsehoods, tantamount to confessions, and his killing of Oswald allow us to draw all these inferences.

Jack Ruby's motive to brazenly lie in the face of five eyewitnesses that Ruby was aware had seen him on the third floor at 7:00 p.m. because he personally knew four of them and had spoken to them, and the motive for Ruby to claim that he wasn't there couldn't be clearer. An armed Ruby, familiar enough with guns to have two prior convictions for carrying a concealed deadly weapon, knew he was looking to get at least one shot off to silence Oswald and was stopped before he could get into the interrogation room. For the man who, less than two days later, would shoot Oswald, there was no other reason for him to try to enter the room than to shoot Oswald. He tried to enter not by knocking but by using the unlocked doorknob.

There was no way Ruby could explain away his intrusion, and so he denied he was at the Dallas Police Department building at all that early evening on Friday. Jack Ruby's simple lie would help him keep a lid on his guilty knowledge. A suspect can get into a bind explaining and opening doors to more explaining. It's so much easier to keep the lie simple. "I wasn't even there at Parkland Hospital. I wasn't even there at the Dallas Police Department at those 7:00 p.m. times that I was seen there by those five eyewitnesses. I didn't get there until 11:15 p.m." And on Saturday we'll see the same simple lie, "I wasn't even there on Saturday."

Despite his denial and despite the Warren Commission's report promoting his lies, Ruby really was on the third-floor hallway early Friday evening when Lee Harvey Oswald said famously on television at 7:55 p.m. that day, "I'm just a patsy." Even if Oswald meant he was the Dallas Police Department's patsy, a scapegoat, his use of that word implying a conspiracy and its on-air repetition throughout the world and well beyond that weekend had to have sealed Oswald's fate with his Mafia co-conspirators. He was in extremely urgent need of silencing, and it likewise sealed Ruby's fate as the designated shooter of Oswald.

A motive to suppress the interrogation can be seen not just on Friday evening when an armed Ruby tried to push into the inter-rogation room, but also on Sunday morning at the very moment Ruby murdered Oswald. When Ruby shot Oswald, at great personal danger to himself, he knew he was stopping any further interrogation and stopping Oswald from ever becoming a cooperating witness like Mafia turncoat Joe Valachi had been just a month prior.

To suppress Victor Robertson as fully as possible, Earl Warren had to suppress all five of the Friday-evening eyewitnesses. To support Jack Ruby's alibi that he was elsewhere than outside Captain Fritz's glass office at 7:00 p.m., all five had to be branded as mistaken about seeing Ruby around 7:00 p.m. All five had to be rendered incapable of telling time or of knowing the difference between the third-floor hallway outside homicide at 7:00 p.m. and the basement conference room at 11:15 p.m.

As for the time period after 11:15 p.m., a period that Ruby admitted to being at the Dallas Police Department, Ruby used a string of laughable excuses to explain his hanging around. He bought deli sandwiches for the night-shift police officers. When he found out the police on duty had eaten, he switched his tactic to trying to track down a KLIF radio employee to get the phone number to deliver deli sandwiches to the radio station. An honest investigator would have been embarrassed to write with approval, as Earl Warren did, *"Though he has said his original purpose was only to locate a KLIF employee, Ruby has stated that while at the police station he was 'carried away with the excitement of history.'"*

While "carried away with the excitement of history," Ruby climbed on a table in the basement conference room during the midnight press conference to either get a better view of Oswald, to be seen by Oswald, or both. In his report Earl Warren takes no notice of the photo of Jack Ruby standing on top of this table, other than to concede that because there is a photo of Jack Ruby standing on the table, head and shoulders above reporters and photographers, and because Jack Ruby admitted to being there at that time, Ruby clearly was there at that time. And that's all there is to that.

To be guilty of a conspiracy, not all of the conspirators need to have had preexisting contact with each other. Only Jack Ruby and Oswald knew whether the two had met in person during the planning stages. By conspicuously standing on that table during the press conference, and five hours earlier by roaming the third-floor hallway through which Oswald was paraded, and by intruding into the office where he easily would have been seen by Oswald through the glass, Ruby knew whether by his face alone he was warning Oswald, Mafia style, that Oswald wasn't safe in jail. The message was that Ruby was keeping an eye on him, had free access to him, and that Oswald had

176

better continue to keep his mouth shut or he, his wife, and their two infant daughters would be killed, Mafia style, with pain.

I once represented a Colombian cocaine dealer whose "keys" (kilos) that he distributed in America came from the Cali cartel. One day while he and I and the DEA agent, Bill Glanz, were in a conference room listening to wiretap tapes, a note was passed into the room. It stated that a lawyer from Miami was there to see me about my client. I left the room and smelled his cologne before I saw him. A lawyer who looked like a wealthier version of the singer Julio Iglesias greeted me. He was dressed like a jet-setting multimillionaire with a soft and creamy burgundy leather briefcase that I still covet. He didn't want to see my client. All he wanted to tell me, as we stood in the brightly polished federal building hallway, was that my client's mother had called him from her home in Cali and retained him to fly from Miami to Delaware to inquire how her son was doing. The lawyer asked me to repeat his words to my client.

Recognizing it as a threat against my client's mother, I said, "Please reassure his mother that he's not cooperating."

"No, no, I didn't mean that," the lawyer with the briefcase lied.

"Tell his mother that we're merely listening to wiretap tapes, and he has no intention of cooperating." That happened to be true. The lawyer left and flew back to Miami, no doubt on his own jet.

Earl Warren's promotion of lie after lie from Jack Ruby's lips required insulting police detectives and news reporters. And there would be more of these insults regarding Saturday's crop of telltale Pinocchio lies.

By easily rehabilitating Mrs. Earlene Roberts as an eyewitness on Friday afternoon and Victor Robertson as an eyewitness on Friday evening, and by adding Ruby's lies about not being at Parkland Hospital on Friday afternoon, not being at the police department, or at the door outside homicide on Friday evening, we have clear proof of a conspiracy comprised of Jack Ruby, Lee Harvey Oswald, and two beeping patrolmen.

On the next day, Saturday, Jack Ruby and the conspirators were no longer hunting for an off-the-cuff opportunity to silence Oswald. They began to formulate a plan to silence Oswald built around his transfer to the sheriff's jail.

The black hand of the Mafia, alluded to so far, will reveal itself completely on Sunday.

CHAPTER THIRTY-THREE

Built Around the Transfer

Earl Warren spent no time at all trying to help his readership understand the significance of Jack Ruby's sleepless itinerary in the hours that followed the Friday midnight press conference. Ruby had pulled an all-nighter.

Until the wee hours of Saturday morning, Jack Ruby stuck close to the available sources of news, just as he had done during the assassination when, after finishing his ads, he sat reading the newspaper at the newspaper office, waiting to hear news of the assassination, and then headed to Parkland Hospital.

Jack Ruby was one of the last to leave the Dallas Police Department basement midnight press conference, having spent two hours there. He then hung out at radio station KLIF, where it was described by a witness that he had "settled in the newsroom for the 2:00 a.m. newscast." A staffer said Ruby "looked rather pale to me as he was talking to me, and he kept looking at the floor."

After he had left the KLIF source of news, Jack Ruby hung out at the *Times Herald* newspaper office for about an hour until 4:30 a.m. At this source of the news Jack Ruby engaged in what he later called "the hilarity of frolicking."

We didn't have news radio in those days, and TV stations signed off every night around midnight. Jack Ruby spent his time after the midnight press conference by trying to catch news of Oswald the only way available to him: by hanging out in two newsrooms all night long. It helped that he was charged up on "prellies," a form of amphetamine.

Less than two days later, on Sunday morning at 11:21, Jack Ruby jumped out from behind a massive policeman named William "Blackie" Harrison and shot Oswald at the only instant in time anyone could have gotten off a clean shot at the target. That was the time of the transfer from the Dallas PD jail to the sheriff's jail. The transfer had begun in the ample basement of the Dallas Police Department. Oswald was required to walk a few steps from the jail door to the transferring vehicle with a detective on either side of him. Because he would be cuffed at the wrist to one of the detectives, Oswald would be upright, making him a standing human target—chest, abdomen, brain, and heart exposed.

Since it happened during the transfer on Sunday morning, a detective's scenario must include the reasonable inference that the whole thing was built around the transfer.

The day prior, on Saturday, a false rumor ran among the media that the transfer would take place that day at 4:00 p.m. The false rumor had been started by Dallas PD Chief Jesse Curry, who announced to the press at noon on Saturday that Oswald "will go to the [sheriff's] jail sometime today."

On Saturday, Dallas PD sergeant D. V. Harkness observed Ruby at the vehicular entrance to the sheriff's jail after 4:00 p.m. when that officer cleared the crowd that had gathered in anticipation of the rumored transfer. Again, proof that the man who murdered Oswald less than twenty-four hours later was there to stalk and murder Oswald to silence him comes from the fact that Ruby lied and denied ever being at the sheriff's jail at any time on Saturday.

On Saturday afternoon at the Dallas Police Department, situated nine blocks from the sheriff's jail, five news reporters saw Jack

Ruby hanging out at the Dallas PD building. Once again, Ruby went up against this batch of five eyewitnesses and denied having been at the Dallas Police Department on Saturday, and once again Chairman Warren proceeded to suppress the testimony of all five of the eyewitnesses.

Earl Warren wrote: *"None of the persons who believed they saw Ruby at the police department on Saturday had known him previously...."*

Well, there goes every liquor store stick-up case out the window. The victim never knows the robber "previously." The professional Earl Warren knew that, for sure.

Like Pinocchio's, Ruby's nose grew longer with each lie.

Two of the five news reporters had had memorable encounters with Jack Ruby on Saturday.

Immediately outside the Dallas Police Department building an NBC television producer named Frederic Rheinstein saw Jack Ruby at that location. The producer was manning a television monitor that displayed the third floor of the Dallas Police Department building. Jack Ruby, described as an annoying "creep" and an "irritant" by the NBC producer, was there looking at the NBC monitor, keeping a watchful eye on the third floor.

Later, while viewing the third-floor monitor, the producer saw Jack Ruby, the annoying "creep," now comfortably patrolling the third floor. This incident took place prior to a scheduled 6:00 police announcement on Saturday evening.

Also on Saturday, four more newsmen saw Ruby in the hallway on the third floor. These were live sightings. The four were Thayer Waldo from nearby Fort Worth, who took a business card from Ruby; Frank Johnston of the UPI; and two reporters from France, Philippe Labro and François Pelou. All these journalists chatted with Ruby. Philippe Labro said that when Ruby learned the reporter was French he said, "Ooh la la, Folies Bergère." These encounters were before 6:00 p.m. Saturday. Ruby denied ever being there. Each time Ruby lied, he added to the evidence that he was out to silence Oswald to protect

SUPPRESSING THE TRUTH IN DALLAS

the Mafia conspiracy, a conspiracy that Earl Warren was simultaneously out to protect.

Saturday at some time around 6:00 p.m. the Dallas Police Department made the important announcement to the press that the transfer to the sheriff's jail would take place the next morning, Sunday at 10:00. Significantly, Jack Ruby was not seen at the Dallas Police Department after that 6:00 p.m. transfer announcement. The reasonable inference is that Ruby, who had been glued to Oswald, had gotten the news of the transfer timing for the next day and no longer needed to stalk Oswald that evening.

Whether Jack Ruby was milling around the Dallas Police Department before 6:00 p.m. that Saturday or whether, as he claimed, he wasn't anywhere near it on Saturday was determined by Earl Warren to be up in the air, a toss-up, despite the French eyewitnesses. In his report Earl Warren wrote: *"The Commission...reached no firm conclusion as to whether or not Ruby visited the Dallas Police Department on Saturday."* That by-now typical Earl Warren conclusion means that Saturday afternoon's five eyewitnesses at the Dallas Police Department, like Friday's five eyewitnesses at the Dallas PD at 7:00 p.m., do not trump Jack Ruby. Ruby rules!

"Stalking," with its *Man Hunt* implications, is the word G. Robert Blakey first applied to Ruby's behavior and has used since.

Once again, Jack Ruby would be lying about the stalking, adding more incriminating evidence through his lies.

Good police work is often very tedious work. Taking Sergeant D. V. Harkness at the sheriff's jail gate, Seth Kantor and Mrs. Wilma Tice at Parkland Hospital, and Mrs. Earlene Roberts at the rooming house, and adding them to the Friday five and the Saturday five, a reader of the Warren Commission report will have seen fourteen eyewitnesses dismissed from the case on the baseless grounds of being wrong about what each had clearly heard and seen and when they had heard and seen it. Chief Justice Earl Warren, the founding father of the suppression of truthful evidence in a state case such as this, suppressed each of the fourteen eyewitnesses.

Fourteen eyewitness dismissed from a single case has to be a record.

In his interrogation in connection with his arrest for shooting and killing Oswald, Jack Ruby admitted that he had spent the early afternoon on Saturday hanging about Dealey Plaza, the site of John F. Kennedy's assassination and conveniently across the street from the sheriff's jail where Ruby could spot any incoming transfer preparations or activity.

Jack Ruby then drove to a parking garage next to his Carousel strip club. At 1:30 p.m. on Saturday, a garage attendant eyewitness overheard Jack Ruby on a pay phone mention "Chief Curry" of the Dallas PD. In his car, Jack Ruby left the garage for a period, returning to the garage at 3:00 p.m. This time he told another attendant that he was "acting like a reporter." According to Earl Warren's report this attendant *"heard Ruby address someone…as 'Ken' and caught portions of a conversation concerning the transfer of Oswald."*

Bells and whistles should go off for any detective hearing *"the transfer of Oswald."* A professional investigator would make mental note of the fact that Jack Ruby, supported in his lies by Earl Warren, claimed in his interrogation after he shot Oswald that he had found himself at the Dallas Police Department at the time of the transfer and the Oswald murder by accident, by a chain of unrelated events, and that he had shot Oswald impulsively out of the emotion of the moment and with no real forethought.

"Ken" was later identified as newsman Ken Dove of KLIF, who testified that he had received both calls from Ruby at the garage on Saturday afternoon.

"Ken" said: *"In one call…Ruby asked whether the station knew when Oswald would be moved."* Indeed, Jack Ruby was desperate to nail down the time of the transfer as that would be the only time he would be able to get within range of shooting Oswald in a vital part of his body.

"Ken" then attributed certain remarks to Jack Ruby that more than anything else demonstrate that the whole plan was built around the transfer. Jack Ruby said to Ken: *"I understand they are moving Oswald to the [sheriff's] jail. Would you like you to cover it? Because I am a pretty good friend of [DA] Henry Wade's and I believe I can get some pretty good news stories."*

That this was left without a single comment by Chairman Warren goes beyond the left shoe on the right foot. Here was Jack Ruby attempting to magically transform himself from a clearly unauthorized person into a credentialed authorized reporter for what, unlike the Friday-evening third-floor "tsunami," would be a secure transfer procedure in the basement of the Dallas Police Department. With credentials, no one would say, "You can't go in there, Jack."

With "press" credentials, "big red ones" pinned to his suit, he would be representing a KLIF newsman, if Ken had agreed. Ruby could lie in wait for his prey in the basement without fear of being prematurely ejected for not having press credentials. He'd use them for an opportunity to kill Oswald.

Ken Dove did not accept this offer. Jack Ruby would remain an unauthorized person at transfer time. And knowing that he wouldn't be credentialed on Saturday in order for him to penetrate the basement of the Dallas Police Department at the rumored 4:00 p.m. transfer time, Jack Ruby showed up at the other end, at the gate of the sheriff's jail, where Sergeant D. V. Harkness observed him as Harkness cleared the crowd at the gate. Jack Ruby was at the gate vainly hoping to get a desperate shot off as the transfer car pulled up to deliver its package, Oswald in the flesh.

That Jack Ruby told a garage attendant that he was *"acting like a reporter"* further corroborated both Detective Eberhardt and reporter John Rutledge, who had seen him doing the reporter routine Friday evening at 7:00 around the time Ruby opened the glass-paneled door to homicide.

Examining Ruby's very own transfer as a murder defendant from the Dallas Police Department to the sheriff's jail following his arrest for murdering Oswald also demonstrates that the murder of Oswald, indeed, was built around the transfer. Jack Ruby knew that the time his bosses determined was the only time anyone could get off a shot at Oswald was at transfer time. That golden moment presented a sliver of an opportunity when Lee Harvey Oswald would be exposed enough to be shot. Jack Ruby knew that if his bosses wanted to silence him, this tactical thinking logically extended to his own transfer time one day following his arrest for murdering Oswald.

Jack Ruby was described by the transfer detectives as "shaking" when he stepped off the elevator to walk through the office to the jail door. When Ruby stepped through the jail door into the underground basement he broke away in a panic. He bolted from his detective escorts, shocking them. He ran at top speed to the awaiting transfer car with its back door open to receive him. Terrified, he flung himself in on hands and knees, lay flat on his belly on the floor, and wouldn't budge. Detective Jim Leavelle, one of the astonished transfer escorts, had to rest his feet on Ruby's petrified body the whole nine blocks to the sheriff's jail. Leavelle said, *"Jack was frightened and that's where he wanted to stay."* To make it even scarier for Ruby, Detective Leavelle, wearing a beige cowboy hat, had been handcuffed to Oswald at the time of his transfer. Ruby was not going to let Leavelle get a cuff on him.

Lying there on his belly with a detective's feet planted on him, Jack Ruby knew the whole thing was built around the transfer, and that worked both ways.

CHAPTER THIRTY-FOUR

The Early Bird

A t 2:30 Sunday morning, nearly eight hours before Oswald's sched-uled transfer, the sheriff's office and the FBI office in Dallas, but curiously not the Dallas Police Department, each received an anony-mous call that a committee of one hundred citizens had voted to kill Oswald *"tonight, tomorrow morning, or tomorrow night…we will be there and we will kill him."*

These two anonymous calls with their schedule of times that Oswald would be killed obviously were themselves also built around the transfer.

All of law enforcement on the case knew that and knew that the only time Oswald could be in a position to be killed was during the transfer. Thus, following those calls, the authorities began to debate whether to transfer Oswald unexpectedly in the middle of the night or to keep to the original transfer timing that could expose Oswald to these vigilantes.

The Secret Service agent in the room, a man whose career was the logistics of protecting individuals during transfers, recommended an immediate nighttime transfer *"at three or four in the morning when there's no one around."*

186

That advice was echoed by the Dallas FBI supervisor Gordon Shanklin, who went so far as to telephone Dallas chief Jesse Curry and repeat his advice in front of his FBI agents. In his book, FBI Special Agent James Hosty, Jr., recounted the conversation:

Chief, this is Gordon Shanklin again. Remember that phone call in which we were...warned that Oswald was to be killed during his transport this morning?... Well, you know that it's my recommendation that you cancel those plans and try something else.... You're still going forward.... Well, I just wanted to warn you again.

Nevertheless, the decision was made by Dallas PD to stick to the announced transfer plan and wait until the morning. A homicide investigator would note the chief's decision to disregard the caller's threats as suspicious.

Had the Secret Service agent's advice been followed, Jack Ruby would have been off the hook with Dallas Mafia boss Joseph Civello, underboss Joe Campisi, and their boss Carlos Marcello. They would have had to come up with a plan to kill Oswald in the sheriff's jail after he got there. The bosses did have a friend in the sheriff's office, the man in charge of the jail, the sheriff himself. The sheriff had once acted as a character reference for Dallas Mafia boss Joseph Civello in a pardon application, the way Peter Bosch, Jimmy Corrigan, and I had for Bobby Golson.

As my Mafia tutors had taught me, a refusal by Ruby to do "a piece of work" ordered by a boss is a death sentence, if you're lucky.

But if the transfer occurred in secret, in the wee hours of the morning, Jack Ruby would have had a valid excuse that could have protected him, his sisters Eva and Eileen, and his brother Earl from murder by torture, Chicago style, as perfected by the notorious Mad Sam DeStefano, a name well-known in the underworld.

Did Jack Ruby make these two anonymous calls? No one can prove or disprove it with evidence the way we have endeavored to do thus far, that is, with proof beyond a reasonable doubt. On this topic of who made these calls, we can only speculate on the scenario. Even a crank caller would know that the Dallas Police Department housed Oswald and that the department was in charge of the case and the transfer, with the FBI in a subordinate role and the sheriff's office having no role. That the Dallas PD, strangely, was not called by the early-bird caller leans toward Jack Ruby as the caller being afraid his voice would be recognized at the Dallas Police Department but not as easily at the sheriff's office or the FBI office.

At any rate, the anonymous calls that almost propelled the transfer team to steal away in the night went unheeded, and the previously announced plan went forward for the transfer on Sunday sometime after 10:00 a.m.

CHAPTER THIRTY-FIVE

Transfer Time

The Oswald transfer took place at 11:21 a.m. on Sunday.

At 11:17 a.m. Jack Ruby was in a Western Union office two hundred steps from the entrance ramp to the Dallas Police Department basement and its jail door through which Oswald would walk out into the basement and into a waiting transfer car.

That Jack Ruby was in that Western Union office sending a money order to a stripper at 11:17 a.m. helped Chairman Warren and others among his loyalists argue that Jack Ruby was cutting it too close to have been planning to silence Oswald in that time frame. Actually, using the Western Union time clock, the time frame included anywhere from 11:17 until the expiration of an additional fifty-nine seconds.

Chairman Warren claimed that, overcome by grief, and happening upon the scene on his way to the Western Union office, Jack Ruby acted alone on the spur of the moment. He just *happened* to have his gun with him.

These claims by Chairman Warren ignore that any transfer timing for Jack Ruby's homicidal purposes had to have been cut razor-close, as it was in the scene Victor Robertson had personally witnessed. As an unauthorized person, easily recognized, Jack Ruby could not be seen in the basement very long before he jumped out from behind the massive police officer William "Blackie" Harrison to open fire. The window for Ruby or anyone else to kill Oswald at transfer time would be open for a matter of seconds, the time it took Oswald to walk from the jail door to the transfer car, while Ruby simultaneously was walking down the entrance ramp as if on a split screen.

Optimally, if he were getting help from the Dallas Police Department, Jack Ruby needed a signal from a policeman at the bottom of the down entrance ramp for him to know when it was time for him to start walking down the entrance ramp. Jack Ruby needed a policeman who was on guard at the top of the down entrance ramp to ignore him walking in and down the ramp. Jack Ruby needed a policeman in the basement to signal prematurely to Captain Fritz and the homicide detectives that all was ready, that it was time to bring Oswald down on the elevator from the third floor, and prematurely that it was time to escort Oswald into the basement to the waiting transfer car. Being heavyset, Jack Ruby needed a large body to hide behind momentarily until Oswald passed through the jail door and stepped into the basement.

Security plans called for the basement to be cleared of unauthorized personnel. Only credentialed press was supposed to be permitted to cover the transfer, but afterwards members of the press said no one was actually checking credentials. To ensure that the transfer was done in safety, every car in the basement was inspected, even police cars in the garage section. All car trunks were opened, and guards were posted. When a phone call from the basement to the third floor confirmed that all was at the ready, Captain Fritz and two detectives, one on either side of Oswald, would escort Oswald down in the elevator to the jail office. When all again was announced to be at the ready, Oswald would be taken out from the jail office, through the jail door, and into the basement. The detective on Oswald's right, Jim Leavelle, in a beige cowboy hat, would be handcuffed to Oswald. Credentialed reporters would be on the other side of the "auto ramp," where a railing would have separated them from Oswald. The transfer car would be in position in a direct line from the jail door to the rear door of the car, which would be opened to receive Oswald for the nine-block trip up the exit ramp and to the sheriff's jail, as later would be done with a frightened and panicky Jack Ruby by Detective Leavelle.

Unlike Ruby's transfer, two lines of police officers were to serve as a human funnel for Oswald and his two detective escorts from the jail door to the door of the transfer car. Oswald and his two escorts would have two lines full of bodies around them for protection, like two lines of conga dancers.

But something went wrong with the security, and trouble began.

As Warren's report admits but makes no effort to explore or explain: *"Fritz was…prematurely informed that the basement arrangements were complete."*

Getting the all-was-at-the-ready signal, the transfer party "prematurely" came down on the elevator to the jail office. For a second time, they were informed "prematurely" that all was at the ready for them to exit the jail office and for them to safely enter the basement through the jail door and walk the few feet to the transfer car sitting at the bottom of the down entrance ramp in a position to go up the exit ramp.

When he marched his prisoner through the jail door into the basement, Detective Leavelle "was surprised" that the transfer car "was not in the spot it should have been." It was still "backing into position." But it had to back up into newsmen who had not been kept in their position.

Leavelle explained: *"The newsmen were not kept east of the auto ramp where a railing would have separated them from Oswald."*

Most importantly, instead of two lines of police bodies funneling and shielding the transfer party, the officers were backed off and up against the wall on either side of the wide hallway leading from the jail door, as if to invite a shooter into the open space. In such a position, the police would have a wall to lean against but would be useless to shield Lee Harvey Oswald, as they indeed were when Jack Ruby jumped out from behind the massive Blackie Harrison, who was in a small crowd improperly gathered at the bottom of the down entrance ramp. From the range of a couple of feet, Ruby shot Oswald once in the abdomen before Ruby was wrestled to the ground and disarmed.

How could so many things go wrong, especially the false "ready" signals on two occasions that all was at the ready for the transfer party—false "ready" signals that delivered Oswald into the preferred range of Ruby's snub-nosed .38?

The officer in charge of security for the transfer specifically had assigned Blackie Harrison. How could Harrison be standing motionless in a small crowd that it was his duty to push back behind the railing?

Jack Ruby stayed to his left closer to that railing going down the eighty-foot entrance ramp. He kept to his left the whole way down. Staying to the left gave Jack Ruby a twenty-five-foot-sooner view of the jail door that Oswald would come out of than if Ruby had stayed to the right, where his view of the jail door would have been blocked by the wall until he got to the end of it. Keeping left to get a better view of the jail door is at least some evidence to corroborate that Jack Ruby was hunting Oswald, that the mission was planned in detail, and the killing of Oswald was not an impulsive act by Jack Ruby. It was a *Man Hunt*.

How did Jack Ruby get down the eighty-foot entrance ramp from Main Street, past the officer there to guard the ramp's entryway, an officer specifically placed there at the top of the ramp by the officer in charge of all the security?

Who was the officer in charge of all the security?

Carlos Marcello did not attend the historic November 1957 Apalachin conference. It was an important conference at the highest level of the Mafia. Marcello sent in his place someone he trusted implicitly, Dallas boss Joseph Civello, to represent him at the conference. When Joseph Civello returned to Dallas from his unpleasant experiences with a New York state police raiding party, Civello was spotted having dinner with Dallas Police Department Sergeant Patrick Dean. Sergeant Dean was a close friend to both Joseph Civello and Jack Ruby.

The police officer in charge of security at Oswald's transfer time was Dallas Mafia boss Joseph Civello's policeman friend, Sergeant Patrick Dean. As head of security for the entire operation, Sergeant Dean had assigned a few men to help him, including Blackie Harrison.

What was ready about "ready?"

Sergeant Patrick Dean was ready when Jack Ruby was ready.

In his report Chairman Warren concluded that Jack Ruby entered into the basement by way of the down entrance ramp from Main Street and was in the basement for no more than three minutes. A CBS TV tape shows Jack Ruby already in the basement and concealed behind the massive body of Blackie Harrison, who was standing at the bottom of the down entrance ramp. Standing in this position, Harrison would have been visible to Jack Ruby from the Main Street–level entryway before Ruby took the first step in his descent down the entrance ramp.

On television, before Ruby's arrival, Blackie is twice seen looking over his shoulder up the ramp while everyone else's eyes are straight ahead on the jail door from which Oswald would soon be emerging.

If Jack Ruby got down the ramp too early and lay in wait for his prey, as a recognizable and unauthorized person, he may well have been spotted and ejected by any honest cop doing his job, especially after the two "vigilante" phone calls warning that Oswald was going to be killed during this transfer.

Jack Ruby needed to be signaled to come down the ramp when all eyes would be on the jail door. And that would be after the transfer party falsely had been given the signal that all was ready for them to come down. I submit that Blackie standing in position at the bottom of the ramp had to have been the signal for Jack Ruby at the top of the ramp to saunter down the ramp and get himself into position behind Blackie. Blackie was too busy being a human shield for Jack Ruby to actually do his job and clear the bottom of the ramp of people who didn't belong there. Besides, the little crowd at the bottom of the ramp would help Jack Ruby conceal himself.

Meanwhile, Sergeant Patrick Dean was looking down on the scene from a high perch on the up exit ramp. As Earl Warren notes, but makes no attempt at explaining, at the time of the shooting, *"Dean was then partway up the...[exit] ramp."*

Blackie claimed that he never saw Jack Ruby standing behind him and to his left. No doubt Blackie directed his gaze away from seeing Ruby, who was practically touching him. Like a comic character in a silent film, William "Blackie" Harrison was all but whistling and looking innocent as he stared off in space. Had Blackie glanced at Ruby right next to him, he would have had to eject him or risk having it caught on film.

As stated, the only possible time a vigilante could kill Oswald was at transfer time, and all the police would know that. Considering that the anonymous calls put the transfer on even higher alert than normal, it borders on the impossible to believe that Blackie Harrison, a handpicked member of Sergeant Patrick Dean's security detail assigned to keep unauthorized persons out of the basement, would fail to inventory everyone in his immediate vicinity were he doing his job. A police officer doing his job especially would have inventoried someone who mysteriously arrived from behind him.

When Blackie Harrison was seen on film twice looking over his shoulder and up the ramp, a reasonable inference can be drawn that Blackie had to have been checking to see if Jack Ruby had arrived.

Another reasonable inference can be drawn from Jack Ruby's selection of Blackie Harrison as the man to position himself behind. Ruby would not have gotten behind just any innocent policeman who might have given him the boot. Harrison had to have been selected for this role, and Ruby had to have known that.

The only eyes easily on the entire down entrance ramp, and therefore on Jack Ruby coming down it, would have been Sergeant Patrick Dean's. Standing halfway up the mirror-opposite exit ramp, Sergeant Dean was in a perfect position to get the benefit of Blackie's signal that Ruby was in launch position on Main Street. Sergeant Dean could then actually see Ruby come down and get into his final position behind Blackie. Any policeman telephoning the third-floor detectives from the basement that all was "ready" to bring Oswald down from the third floor and then signaling that it was safe to bring Oswald out through the jail door had a clear view of Sergeant Dean on high signaling "prematurely."

Sergeant Dean was conducting more than traffic that morning. Dean was like a shooter of clay pigeons calling out, "Pull!"

Would anyone want Mafia boss Joseph Civello's friend Sergeant Dean in charge of security at transfer time? Would anyone want Dean on a perch high above the transfer scene? Seth Kantor claimed that the Dallas Police Department was "rotten from top to bottom." Here it was rotten from the top of the ramp to the bottom of the ramp.

When later summoned for questioning, Blackie Harrison reported to the Warren Commission accompanied by a lawyer. In those days that was a recognized sign of guilt. An honest policeman on the department who worked organized crime, Lieutenant Jack Revill, made it known that he suspected Blackie Harrison of conspiring with Jack Ruby and helping Ruby get down the ramp. This accusation made Lieutenant Revill a very unpopular man among certain officers in the Dallas PD.

The transfer timing had to be as good as the Mafia always made such things, and it was.

Since everyone would be ready only when Jack Ruby was ready, Ruby even had a little time to spare at the Western Union office a block from the Dallas Police Department. Ruby sent a hard-up stripper a time-stamped $25 money order. In addition to his .38, Ruby had brass knuckles in his pocket. Four minutes later he was yelling at the policemen who jumped him and arrested him, *"You guys all know me. I'm Jack Ruby."*

Before Ruby went into the Western Union office, when he parked his car in a parking lot at about 11:15 a.m., he put his billfold in his trunk, locked the trunk, and then put the trunk key in his glove compartment. What was his reason for doing that in the circumstances of this public execution of Oswald? I found only one author who even mentioned the billfold going into the trunk, and that was Vincent Bugliosi. He simply called it "odd."

Rather than merely "odd," it was a habit by a man who had done other hits or crimes of violence like truck hijackings or stick-ups. Such a man doesn't want his billfold slipping out of his pocket during the crime, especially if a scuffle erupted. Under the impact of his assignment, Ruby resorted to his normal routine. Putting his billfold away was a dead giveaway that his billfold needed protection in action that he knew was about to happen. Locking his billfold in his trunk and hiding the trunk key in his glove compartment is solid evidence that this murder of Oswald was not a spontaneous act by a brokenhearted Ruby but was planned and premeditated.

It was the Case of the Telltale Billfold.

In his report Warren assured the public: *"The Dallas Police Department, concerned at the failure of its security measures, conducted an extensive investigation that revealed no information indicating complicity between any police officer and Jack Ruby."* The Dallas Police cleared the Dallas Police, and Earl Warren cleared them both. And that was that.

CHAPTER THIRTY-SIX

A Messenger On a Mission

In its biography section on Jack Ruby, Earl Warren's report painted Ruby as mostly a crybaby mental case instead of the tough Chicago customer he was. Warren did concede, however, that Ruby routinely beat up people, including women, using brass knuckles, blackjacks, pistol whippings, and foot stompings, and made his victims crawl out of his club on their hands and knees.

But Jack Ruby did love his siblings and was especially close to his sister Eva, who managed his Vegas Club, and his brother Earl.

A scant few days after his arrest for killing Oswald, and after his own transfer from the Dallas Police jail to the sheriff's jail, Jack Ruby had his first visitor. Joe Campisi was the Dallas underboss to Joseph Civello and the future Dallas boss. Campisi was the owner of the Egyptian Lounge, where Jack Ruby had eaten dinner the night before the assassination. As they ate, they must have known what was going to happen the next day. When Joe Campisi arrived at the sheriff's jail, he told Jack Ruby that the sheriff in charge of the jail, who had once helped Mafia boss Joe Civello get a pardon, had asked him to visit.

Fifteen years later Joe Campisi would freely repeat this admission to Professor Blakey's House Select Committee. On this visit,

Campisi needed to make no threats to Jack Ruby. His mention of the sheriff, the Dallas boss Joseph Civello's friend and pardon *supporter*, was threat enough against Jack Ruby concerning his safety in the sheriff's jail, and Campisi's face was threat enough against Eva, Eileen, and Earl.

Campisi's visit was actually to deliver a mortal threat. He was a messenger on a mission. As well, Campisi would later attend at least part of Jack Ruby's murder trial.

As anyone professionally knowledgeable about the Mafia would know, another reason for Campisi to show his face was to reassure Jack Ruby that as long as he behaved himself, his family and his businesses would be taken care of financially.

At a crucial point in Earl Warren's investigation for his only client, "the truth," Jack Ruby begged Warren to transfer him from the sheriff's jail in Dallas to a jail in Washington, DC, where he claimed he'd be freer to tell the truth. Jack Ruby said, point-blank, to Earl Warren, *"Unless you get me to Washington you cannot get a fair shake out of me."*

Warren denied this apparently simple and more-than-reasonable request. Maybe Jack Ruby just wanted to get out from under the sheriff's clutches and wouldn't have confessed in any meaningful way because of concern for the safety of sisters Eva and Eileen and brother Earl, but what was the harm in granting that transfer?

Clearly, in Earl Warren's eyes, the harm in moving Ruby to Washington was that it would make Ruby too accessible to people on the Warren Commission, like former Philadelphia Assistant DA Arlen Specter, who might take it upon themselves to do a little freelance interrogating. It was legal then.

That single request for a transfer to Washington, DC, constitutes the start of a Jack Ruby confession. It means: I have been lying to you. You have not been getting a "fair shake out of me" and you won't until you transfer me. Only then you will get the truth.

Earl Warren gave an ice-cold shoulder to the offer of a confession and its implications. For sure, Senator James Eastland would have transferred Ruby to Beverly Hills and would have cross-examined him at length on the many issues contained in the phrase "fair shake out of me."

It was in that same June 1964 interview by Earl Warren at the sheriff's jail that Jack Ruby said regarding his request to be transferred to Washington: *"Maybe certain people don't want to know the truth that may come out of me."*

Jack Ruby was at that instant a sitting duck for an interrogation leading to a confession, and Earl Warren would know that. Warren would already know from Ruby's trembling transfer drive with Detective Leavelle's feet on his back that Ruby did not trust his bosses not to kill him. By Ruby's actions during his transfer everyone would know that all loyalty was gone and that Ruby needed to look out for himself as Valachi had.

Unfortunately, Jack Ruby was right about "certain people" not wanting the truth, and he was looking at them as he spoke. Ruby's offer of a "fair shake" in exchange for a transfer of prisons must have made Warren's insides shiver, quake, and shudder. By this offer of a "fair shake," Ruby made himself into "a disposal problem."

Not permitted by Earl Warren to attend that June 1964 interview in Dallas were the two commission staff lawyers who had been assigned to investigate Jack Ruby: Leon Hubert and Hubert's partner, Burt Griffin. Warren had dodged a bullet by Hubert and Griffin not hearing Ruby tell Warren that he had not been giving Warren's commission a "fair shake." For sure had they been present they would have jumped all over Ruby on the "fair shake" issue. It was a cross-examination waiting to happen, coming from a more-than-willing witness.

Leon Hubert, as noted, resigned shortly after this meeting with Ruby and Warren because of Earl Warren's interference in Leon Hubert's attempts to investigate Jack Ruby's ties to organized crime in Cuba.

Hubert's partner, Burt Griffin, was the staffer in charge of interviewing Jack Ruby's friend, the man in charge of security in the basement during the transfer, Sergeant Patrick Dean. After Sergeant

Dean's interview, Burt Griffin sat Dean down and accused him of lying in two important ways. Obviously, the interrogation of Sergeant Dean had entered the all-important accusatory stage. Griffin asked Sergeant Dean to reconsider his testimony and to return with a lawyer.

The first suspected lie by Sergeant Dean came from him telling Burt Griffin inconsistent versions of a claim made by Dean. He had claimed that on his arrest Jack Ruby had said that he first thought of shooting Oswald during the Friday midnight press conference. The hunch by Burt Griffin, that Sergeant Dean was lying, was right on the money.

The second accusation of a lie told by Sergeant Dean was even more significant. Griffin accused Dean of, from his exit ramp perch, watching Jack Ruby walk down the entrance ramp and doing nothing to stop Ruby, not even shouting at Ruby to freeze.

Sergeant Patrick Dean did not report back to Burt Griffin with a lawyer. Instead, he reported Burt Griffin's accusations of lying to President Johnson's friend and ally, Dallas District Attorney Henry Wade. DA Wade called President Johnson, who promptly brought Earl Warren in to fix this. Warren straightaway sided with Sergeant Dean and decided to suppress Burt Griffin's accusations that Dean twice had committed perjury during his interview with Griffin. Warren shipped Burt Griffin back to Washington, where he remained, forbidden to question any Dallas police officer ever again. Burt Griffin appears to have been the first law enforcement victim of Earl Warren's *Miranda* mute button that would be created by him two years later. Warren pressed the mute button, and Burt Griffin was silenced.

Sergeant Dean, unlike Jack Ruby, was taken to Washington to testify and to receive a direct public apology from Chairman Earl Warren: *"No member of our staff has a right to tell any witness that he is lying or that he is testifying falsely. That is not his business."* That could not have been lost on the entire staff of innocent young lawyers who didn't need their careers in Washington ruined at the outset.

Another deliberately missed opportunity by Earl Warren was his failure to follow up on the brief FBI interrogation by Special Agent C. Ray Hall. The Hall interrogation had taken place three hours after Jack Ruby silenced Oswald. As noted, a phrase used by Jack Ruby, that as of the time of the shooting, Oswald "had not confessed," added to Victor Robertson's evidence that Jack Ruby shot Oswald to silence him.

In full, Jack Ruby told Special Agent C. Ray Hall of the FBI this obvious untruth about his decision to shoot Oswald: *"If he had confessed to shooting the president, I probably would never have even shot him."*

"Why is that?" Agent Hall asked.

"...since he hadn't confessed I was afraid he might be turned loose."

This opens up a fertile line of proof that Earl Warren completely ignored.

How would Ruby know at transfer time at 11:21 a.m. that Oswald hadn't confessed? Who was giving Jack Ruby information that Saturday evening or in the interrogation held that very Sunday morning that Oswald "hadn't confessed"?

Any professional interrogator would have in his scenario that Jack Ruby was kept abreast of the status of Oswald's cooperation by the Dallas Police Department's Mafia connection, Sergeant Dean, while Jack Ruby sat by the phone until he got his instructions on the transfer timing. Ruby knew that Oswald "hadn't confessed" because it was his life-or-death business to know.

The absurdity of the lie that Ruby killed Oswald out of fear that Oswald would beat the rap, "that he might be turned loose," gives rise to still more evidence from Ruby's mouth, as if any more is needed, that by his lies, Ruby was covering up his real motive to silence Oswald, and Earl Warren had given Jack Ruby a license to lie, like 007's license to kill.

CHAPTER THIRTY-SEVEN

The Ace

Facing trial for first-degree murder, Jack Ruby ended up with the gift of a lawyer he could never have afforded. Ruby's high-priced lawyer was none other than the most prestigious and talented trial lawyer in America at that time, the legendary Swiss Italian American Melvin Belli of San Francisco, the Mafia lawyer with a loaded cannon on his roof.

In his autobiography, *Melvin Belli: My Life on Trial* (Morrow, 1976), Belli wrote glowingly of his close friendship with the notorious Jewish mobster Mickey Cohen, who was the top figure in the Mafia in Los Angeles. Mickey Cohen was the former bodyguard to Bugsy Siegel who, at the time of his murder by the Mafia, was the manager of the Mafia's Flamingo Hotel and Casino. As noted, the Flamingo owners were employers of Justice William O. Douglas and had the judge on retainer.

In the manner in which Dallas was under New Orleans's jurisdiction, Los Angeles was under Chicago's jurisdiction, and since the days of Al Capone the Chicago outfit was multicultural. Italians often stood on equal footing with Irish gangsters, with a well-known Welsh gangster, German gangsters, and Jewish gangsters.

In fact, the Jewish Jack Ruby's best friend growing up in Chicago was the Jewish gangster Lenny Patrick, a suspect in at least two murders, including the murder of a gangster rival that left Lenny Patrick in control of a lucrative bookmaking wire service.

In his 1976 autobiography, Melvin Belli wrote about his dear friend Mickey Cohen as if he were family: *"Cohen...was a gentleman of great courtliness and charm. My little boy...took to Cohen as to the loving grandfather he never met."*

In 1958 during my senior year in high school, the glamorous actress Lana Turner's teenage daughter Cheryl Crane stabbed to death Johnny Stompanato, the enforcer for Mickey Cohen, the "gentleman of great courtliness and charm." Stompanato was Lana Turner's hunk of burning love, but he liked to beat Lana, and one day her daughter came to the rescue. The fatal stabbing was ruled "justifiable homicide."

John Buntin, author of the parallel biographies of Mickey Cohen and the legendary Los Angeles PD chief William Parker, *L.A. Noir* (Broadway, 2010), wrote that in 1972 when Mickey Cohen finished an eleven-year sentence in Springfield, Missouri, for tax evasion, Mickey Cohen's brother picked him up in a new white Cadillac. Instead of driving west to Los Angeles from Springfield, Cohen's brother drove south to New Orleans to spend time with Carlos Marcello, to pay his respects. In Senate Rackets Committee testimony Mickey Cohen said about this trip he took upon his release: *"We talked about the old times, among other things."*

Thirteen years earlier during a McClellan Senate hearing in 1959, Mickey Cohen had described Carlos Marcello to chief counsel Robert F. Kennedy as *"a beautiful person, a real gentleman...."*

Chief Counsel Robert F. Kennedy asked Cohen to explain what it meant when somebody's "lights are to be put out."

"Lookit," said Cohen, *"I don't know what you're talking about. I'm not an electrician."*

The old adage that you're known by the company you keep has no greater meaning than with the exclusive club of the Mafia. Melvin

Belli connected to Mickey Cohen connected to Carlos Marcello makes Belli and his loud cannon in San Francisco "big connected" to Carlos Marcello, the godfather of Dallas.

In 1961 Mickey Cohen sustained another tax evasion conviction and was sent to Alcatraz, then the harshest federal prison in America. Cohen became the only prisoner ever to be bailed out of Alcatraz. Mickey Cohen's release bond was signed by Chief Justice Earl Warren.

Some authors criticize Mickey Cohen's mouthpiece Melvin Belli for his legal defense of Jack Ruby in attempting to sell the jury on a mental illness psychiatric plea. It would have freed Jack Ruby completely if Belli had won. But more importantly for Belli's real clients, his Mafia friends, a psychiatric defense would have proven once and for all to the world that Jack Ruby was a "lone nut," and not part of any Mafia conspiracy, not someone the Mafia would even do business with, a fruitcake.

Belli told Ruby: *"Jack, we're going to do everything in court to show you as the nut that you are."*

On the surface it looked like a big gamble because it would carry the death penalty if the psychiatric defense failed. On the other hand, a guilty plea to "murder without malice," which many of the local experts believed would have been an easy plea, would have given Jack Ruby a five-year sentence. Unfortunately for Ruby, Melvin Belli couldn't use both defenses at the same time, and he chose the psychiatric defense. Ruby, of course, would agree to whatever defense the Mafia lawyer wanted. At Ruby's trial, which began in February 1964, three months after President Kennedy's assassination, Melvin Belli called psychiatric experts to testify, but the jury didn't find them trustworthy, and Belli lost the case. Losing the mental-illness psychiatric defense automatically resulted in Jack Ruby getting a death-penalty sentence for the first-degree murder of Lee Harvey Oswald. Melvin Belli was accused by many of turning a five-year sentence for a sure case of "murder without malice" into a death sentence for Jack Ruby.

However, as the facts unfolded, it was seen that all the while, Melvin Belli was holding an ace in the hole. He could afford to gamble on a mental-illness psychiatric defense. If he had won, Jack Ruby would walk, and the Mafia would be happy that Ruby would forever be known as a head case who had killed Oswald on his own because of his mental illness. If Belli lost the psychiatric defense, the Mafia would still be nearly as happy because of the media exposure of Ruby as a diagnosed head case.

If Melvin Belli lost the head-case ploy, as he did, he would then use his ace in the hole. With a snap of his fingers, Belli would have the conviction overturned on appeal, and the next time around his client would be able to plead "murder without malice." Then Ruby would do five years standing on his head. This was bold, but this was Belli, a "big connected" lawyer.

What was Melvin Belli's ace in the hole?

Texas had a strict prohibition against the use at trial of incriminating statements made by a suspect during interrogation unless the statements were in writing and signed by the suspect. This purely Texas rule was not much of a challenge for a skilled interrogator. Once the cat was out of the bag and the suspect had confessed, he was defeated and would normally sign the handwritten synopsis of the confession prepared by the interrogator.

An exception to the requirement that confessions needed to be signed was for statements made during the arrest that were not the product of police questioning. Such statements not signed and not in writing freely could be introduced at trial.

Melvin Belli had in his pocket an arresting officer from the basement transfer who would testify, seemingly, against Jack Ruby. The officer swore that Ruby claimed he first thought of killing Oswald at Friday's midnight press conference where Ruby had stood on a table. Ruby's planning to kill Oswald two days in advance of the killing would be premeditated murder and would destroy a psychiatric defense.

It would be a great strategy for Belli, however unethical, to have this ace in the hole testify for the prosecution, seemingly against Ruby on this crucial matter of a spontaneous admission made during arrest that was not the product of interrogation. However, when the ace-in-the-hole officer concluded his trial testimony by adding that the statement was made "upstairs," that is, during interrogation in Room 317 following Ruby's arrest in the basement, it was already too late to cure. From the ace-in-the-hole witness, the jury had heard Ruby's confession that he first thought about killing Oswald at the midnight press conference and that he had a gun in his pocket at the time. Once the word "upstairs" was used by the ace in the hole, the officer's testimony guaranteed a sure-thing reversal of the conviction on appeal, which is what happened. Melvin Belli had had a free shot at a complete acquittal at trial, got to put on an infomercial for the Mafia on the subject of Ruby's lack of mental stability, and was gambling nothing.

After his high court victory on appeal a grateful Jack Ruby sent the ace-in-the-hole Dallas policeman an autographed copy of the Warren Commission report, inscribing it: "Your buddy, Jack Ruby."

That ace-in-the-hole "buddy" of Jack Ruby was Sergeant Patrick Dean.

The Warren Commission staff lawyer Burt Griffin, during his interview of Sergeant Dean, had excellent instincts and very good reasons not to believe what later became Sergeant Dean's trial testimony. Not suspecting for a second that his diligence would get him in trouble with Earl Warren and get him banished from the city of Dallas, Burt Griffin confronted Sergeant Dean when Dean couldn't repeat his statement the same way twice. At trial he only had to tell it one time. And at that, after being prepared by the nation's foremost trial lawyer. Sergeant Dean was an ace up Melvin Belli's sleeve, and that was Jack Ruby's ace in the hole.

Who set off that loud cannon blast on Montgomery Street?

Fifteen years later in 1978, Sergeant Patrick Dean told a Dallas newspaper that he had lined up Melvin Belli to represent him in case Professor G. Robert Blakey's House Select Committee on Assassinations were to subpoena him. The committee's funds had run out and its term ended before it could subpoena and interrogate Sergeant Dean.

While in a Texas jail waiting for his new "murder without malice" trial, Jack Ruby personified a nagging potential complication for Chief Justice Warren. Ruby was, as Allen Dulles had labeled the Cuban exiles in the Bay of Pigs Invasion, "a disposal problem." Ruby had expressed a desire to confess if only he were moved to Washington, DC. Naturally, Warren couldn't afford for that to happen. Warren was experienced with criminals and their desires to confess. If that happened, the cover would come off the cover-up, the Mafia would be exposed, and they would in turn expose CONTAC. The next to be exposed would be Operation Mongoose. Eventually would come Mosaddegh in Iran, Arbenz in Guatemala, Trujillo in the Dominican Republic, Lumumba in the Congo, and our allies the Diem brothers in Saigon.

Earl Warren had to think, what if this desire by Ruby to confess, to give the authorities a "fair shake," got out of hand in the boredom and fear of prison life? For how many years would Warren have to live with this "fair shake" threat hanging over his head? Did he wince every time he heard the name Joe Valachi? Jack Ruby was only fifty-one and in apparent good health when he murdered Oswald.

What if Captain Will Fritz decided to visit Jack Ruby in the Texas jail, established a rapport, gained the trust of Ruby, and got him to unburden himself? After all, it was a Dallas case, not a federal case. What if Ruby sent word to Captain Fritz through a fellow inmate that a visit would be worthwhile and very revealing? What if Jack Ruby said he was ready to give Captain Fritz a "fair shake"? How could a professional like Fritz resist such an invitation? What if Fritz got Ruby moved to a safer jail, not under the thumb of the sheriff and Civello and Campisi?

What if Representative Gerald Ford dropped in on Ruby to follow up his line of questioning that Warren had rudely cut off about Ruby's connections in Cuba, and Ruby spilled all the Cuban beans to Ford?

What if legal staffer Leon Hubert dropped in on Ruby to explore Ruby's ties to Cuba, the topic Hubert was forbidden to explore, and over which treatment by Warren caused Hubert to resign?

What if Hubert's partner, the legal staffer Burt Griffin, decided to drop in on Ruby as Joe Campisi had? What if Griffin and Hubert held some resentment toward the "brusque" Earl Warren that compelled them to try their hands at questioning the man they had been assigned to interrogate but were forbidden to? What if Griffin and Hubert were outraged that Sergeant Dean and Melvin Belli had rigged the Ruby case to create a preplanned guaranteed acquittal on appeal, a fix? What if Griffin and Hubert held a deep resentment at not having been permitted to even attend Ruby's interrogation by Warren? Surely they had learned that Ruby begged to be transferred to Washington in exchange for the truth.

What if the ambitious Arlen Specter decided to take a shot at interrogating Ruby? Who wouldn't want to crack the crime of the century?

What if Ruby, not a very balanced person, simply got lonely in jail, as often happens, and cracked? Warren could end up exposed as a fraud, and a fixer. Warren had already endured a severe blow to his reputation from Korematsu. Could he withstand an even worse series of blows as his cover-ups unraveled? Would he be able to keep public congressional investigations from forming?

Knowing how vulnerable he was to these many young and idealistic lawyers, Chief Justice Warren came up with his own ace in the hole to keep Ruby's lips from leaking and sinking the ship.

On June 19, 1966, Chief Justice Earl Warren got together with his chief collaborators Justice William O. Douglas, then still on an annual payroll of close to ten thousand dollars derived from the Mafia's Flamingo Hotel and Casino, and Lyndon Johnson's appointed advisor and Supreme Court justice Abe Fortas. Fortas was then on an annual payroll of $130,000, provided by the securities crook Louis Wolfson who, in violation of the Canons of Ethics' rules against conflicts of interest, had a significant case pending before the Supreme Court. These three professional "sappers and miners"— Warren, Douglas, and Fortas, who would soon resign under threat of impeachment, while Douglas was forced to surrender his Mafia job—aided by two other justices, created a five-vote majority. Earl Warren wrote the decision. This five-vote majority put to use Warren's methodology to create the *Miranda* mute button that silences police questions when the button is pushed. Despite public perception, the *Miranda* case is not really about the reading of rights to a suspect. That part is incidental. The case and its offspring are all about the mute button of "lawyering up."

Earl Warren wrote: *"If the individual states that he wants an attorney, the interrogation must cease...."*

This is Chief Justice Warren's *Miranda* 101. Now we will see the wicked way in which he used it.

After the mute button's creation on June 19, 1966, neither Captain Will Fritz nor any other concerned law enforcement officer would dare approach Jack Ruby in jail because he already had a lawyer, Melvin Belli. To ask a single question of Ruby would get the interrogator in trouble. As detectives said in those early days of the criminal law revolution, "I didn't do the crime, why should I do the time?"

Since his arrest, Ruby had been "lawyered up." Since *Miranda*, none of those potential interrogators, such as Fritz or Griffin, would venture to ask Ruby a single question. He was in custody, and he had a lawyer.

Never again would Earl Warren have to be worried that Jack Ruby might get a visitor and confess as he had wanted to do in June 1964. When lingering under a death sentence and suspecting that Warren didn't really want the truth from him, Ruby nevertheless had offered to give Earl Warren a "fair shake."

Perhaps America's weakest moment in the eyes of the world's law enforcement was the "not guilty" verdict in the O. J. Simpson case. No interrogation was allowed from the moment Simpson slit the throats of two defenseless people. The perfect time to interrogate Simpson would have been the moment he stepped out of the white Bronco after his attempted escape. O. J. was in possession of cash, a wig, a handgun, and his passport. Simpson knew he was done for. My grandmother Rosa could have gotten an immediate confession: "O-a Jay-a, what-a that-a Jezebel-a do to you?"

His crying answer would have been: "Oh, Mama Rosa, she drove me to it."

The police were not allowed to ask him a thing, not even, "O. J., how was the Bronco ride?"

Six months after Ruby gained his *Miranda* rights mute button, he got pneumonia and was admitted to Parkland Hospital on December 9, 1966. There it was discovered that he had lung, liver, and brain cancer. Jack Ruby died from a complication of the lung cancer less than a month later on January 3, 1967, in Parkland Hospital. According to the doctors, Jack Ruby could not have known that he had cancer when he killed Lee Harvey Oswald four years earlier in November 1963, nor when he pleaded with Earl Warren to remove him to Washington, DC, to take his offered confession, his "fair shake," in June 1964. Nor did anyone know of his cancer when Earl Warren turned him into a murderer immune from interrogation, a man who thenceforth would not be able to be persuaded to give any interrogator "a fair shake" or a deathbed confession, as I got from Frank Sheeran and reported in *I Heard You Paint Houses* (Steerforth, 2004).

Unfortunately for the public, and for those professional homicide investigators, such as Captain Will Fritz, who might have wanted to pay Jack Ruby a visit at Parkland Hospital in December 1966 to coax a deathbed confession out of him, Chief Justice Earl Warren's intercession earlier that same year had made it impossible.

And that's the wicked way in which Earl Warren invented *Miranda* to silence a potential interrogator.

CHAPTER THIRTY-EIGHT

Interrogation Interrupted

It cannot be overstated that Jack Ruby shooting Lee Harvey Oswald in cold blood in front of eighty million eyewitnesses glued to live black-and-white television is the most powerful evidence of the Mafia conspiracy to kill President Kennedy. That .38-caliber blast interrupted a good old-fashioned professional interrogation for all time. Interrogation interrupted. This is what the American public saw at the time and still sees. According to the latest polls nearly three-quarters of the nation do not believe Lee Harvey Oswald acted alone in assassinating President John F. Kennedy. The 25 percent who do believe Oswald acted alone weren't necessarily "born yesterday." Many are merely trusting amateurs like Buckley and Mailer.

As seen from Sergeant Dean's ace-in-the-hole testimony, Texas had its own *Miranda*-type rules regarding suspects' confessions. But unlike the national *Miranda* rules, which began emasculating interrogation in America on June 19, 1966, and have continued tightening up interrogation rules ever since, the Texas rule didn't automatically interrupt interrogation forever once a suspect asked for a lawyer. In 1963, three years before *Miranda*, Lee Harvey Oswald repeatedly was questioned despite "lawyering up." He was allowed to consult any lawyer he chose, even a Twelfth Street communist such as John Abt, and to see any lawyer that showed. But when the lawyer left the room the interrogation resumed.

Earl Warren deprived America of that. Lee Harvey Oswald clutched in his murderous hands no *Miranda* mute button to permanently interrupt his interrogation and mute any police questioning.

The Dallas Police Department had a master interrogator in the man described by other Dallas Police officers as "one hundred percent honest." He was the aforementioned chief of homicide, Captain Will Fritz. Had Ruby not killed Oswald, once Oswald was transferred to the peace and quiet of the sheriff's jail Captain Fritz would have used his good stuff on Oswald, leisurely. The communist Oswald was a very opinionated young man, and I know from occasionally going to Stanley's bar on Twelfth Street that communists like to hear themselves talk. This young man with an above-average IQ would be lonely for intelligent conversation.

I'd have paid admission to watch Captain Fritz at work, slowly building a rapport for the journey from establishing trust to unburdening guilt. FBI agent James Hosty was present during part of the ongoing interrogation of Oswald. In his book *Assignment: Oswald*, Hosty wrote about Fritz's impeccable technique:

> *As any cop knows, you always want to keep a suspect talking....*
> *Fritz was speaking to Oswald in the smoothest, most peaceful drawl*
> *he could manage.... Fritz came across as the quintessential southern*
> *good old boy. He had a soft-spoken approach, and his style proved*
> *extremely effective; in fact, Fritz had a much-deserved reputation as*
> *a successful interrogator of homicide suspects, frequently getting both*
> *confessions and convictions.*

Meanwhile, in the third-floor hallway and at the midnight press conference, there may have been an ulterior motive regarding why the Dallas Police Department paraded Oswald before the television cameras. With Texas's state rule governing the admissibility of confessions, the homicide detectives may have seen an opportunity to get an admissible nugget of some kind from Oswald. If Oswald answered a reporter's question, whatever he answered didn't have to be in writing or signed in order to be used against him, such as calling himself "a patsy."

CHAPTER THIRTY-NINE

The Man with No Eyebrows

From his reputation and his successes, Captain Will Fritz clearly was an interrogator's interrogator, like the fictional interrogator Lou Razzi in my detective novel, *The Right to Remain Silent*. Unfortunately, Fritz was an interrogator interrupted in the midst of the masterpiece of his career.

Captain Will Fritz got cheated, and so did posterity. Americans got a decades-long muddle smack in the collective face.

Captain Fritz's notes of his interrogation sessions with Oswald under near-impossible circumstances, with others chiming in and clouding Fritz's atmosphere of quiet trust, are reproduced in the appendix to the Warren Commission report. The notes reveal a policeman who believes we are all God's children. At no time did he look down on the unfortunately fatherless Lee Harvey Oswald. Had it not been for Jack Ruby's killing of Oswald, Captain Fritz would have done his part to allow the turmoil that was Lee Harvey Oswald to finally find a few peaceful days in the end.

The Russian émigré friend of Marina and Lee Harvey Oswald, Jeanne de Mohrenschildt, said about Oswald: *"He might not have become involved in the assassination if people had been kinder to him."*

As Captain Fritz expressed in his notes, he would have been *"more apt to get a confession from [Oswald] if I could have...quietly talked to him."* A confession, of course, would have led to more conspirators whose interrogations would have led to more evidence as the Mafia and CIA CONTAC plot unraveled and the felony murders and first-degree murders came "up to us."

However, Jack Ruby forever silenced all lines of questioning of Oswald by the honest and sincere Captain Will Fritz. The practical effect of Ruby's liquidation of Oswald foreshadowed the *Miranda* ruling's mute button of 1966. *Miranda* was to be a cannon blast fired on the voters without their consent, one that would keep repeating over and over, much to the benefit of Melvin Belli and his clients.

Justice Byron "Whizzer" White was a collegiate football star who went on to law school. President John F. Kennedy appointed White to the United States Supreme Court. The "Whizzer" was to be in the minority in the 1966 *Miranda* decision, dissenting from what Chief Justice Earl Warren and his crew were doing to favor "robbers" and to keep Ruby far away from those to whom Ruby might want to give a "fair shake."

As Associate Justice White put it in his dissent: Miranda's *"next victims are as yet unborn."*

The morning that Jack Ruby shot Lee Harvey Oswald from out of the shadow of Sergeant Dean's buddy Blackie Harrison, two eyewitnesses came forward to authorities in New Orleans, not Dallas.

The eyewitnesses knew that Carlos Marcello's pilot Dave Ferrie, a man with no eyebrows due to his suffering from alopecia, hated President Kennedy for his apparent mishandling of the Bay of Pigs Invasion that led to the slaughter of so many defenseless young men.

One of the eyewitnesses to come forward was a police informant, and the other was a childhood friend of Lee Harvey Oswald. They came forward, unknown to each other and independent of one another, to reveal that the late Lee Harvey Oswald had a personal relationship with Carlos Marcello's pilot, investigator, and friend,

Dave Ferrie. These witnesses knew enough to know that Oswald and Ferrie's relationship needed to be reported to the authorities.

Ferrie was a former Eastern Air Lines pilot. Jimmy Hoffa had fingered Ferrie to Frank Sheeran in 1974 as taking part in a 1963 delivery to Dallas of a duffel bag with three to four rifles sometime prior to assassination weekend. Without looking in the bag or even handling it, Sheeran suspected that the rifles he delivered to an airstrip in Baltimore, in an errand-boy role, were for the contingency that there might be additional routes for the rifles as backup. But this was just a guess, as reported by Sheeran in *I Heard You Paint Houses*.

A documentary I watched about three years into my research, on November 21, 2015, on the American Heroes Channel called *Capturing Oswald*, supplied the answer to the secret of the perceived need for backup rifles in President Kennedy's assassination.

Detective Jim Leavelle was the Dallas police officer in the beige cowboy hat to whom Oswald was handcuffed at the time of his murder. Detective Leavelle explained in the documentary: *"They had laid out three or four routes to take..."* for the president's motorcade.

Hence, the possible need for four high-powered rifles.

This gives rise to an inference based on the evidence thus far that Sergeant Patrick Dean, head of the Dallas Police Department security detail of Oswald, and ace-in-the-hole planted witness for Melvin Belli, had revealed to his Mafia co-conspirators that there were as many as four possible routes that the motorcade could take. It gives rise to an inference that the motorcade route that was selected in the days prior to the event also had been revealed to his Mafia co-conspirators by that same someone, Sergeant Dean. The route selected was Oswald's route, his responsibility, and Oswald had his own rifle with which he was comfortable.

Both of the new eyewitnesses who came forward to law enforcement in New Orleans immediately after Ruby had shot Oswald in Dallas were to reveal that a teenaged Lee Harvey Oswald had been in the New Orleans chapter of the Civil Air Patrol in 1955 and that professional airline pilot Dave Ferrie was Oswald's commander in the patrol.

For even an amateur sleuth, question after question about Oswald's connection to Dave Ferrie, to the Civil Air Patrol, and to Carlos Marcello should "come up to us."

But Earl Warren was "careful." Warren and his commission asked neither of the two Civil Air Patrol witnesses any of these indispensable questions.

Edward Voebel appeared on television stating that he was a childhood friend of Oswald's. Voebel's television appearances forced Chairman Warren to acknowledge his existence in the Warren report and to have him interviewed. Warren, who devoted one paragraph to the golden witness, Earlene Roberts, has two pages that refer to information from Edward Voebel. Voebel described Oswald and himself as having had a "mild friendship." Warren followed up: *"His only close friendship, with Voebel, arose when Voebel helped him tend his wounds after a fight."* Voebel countered about his friend Oswald: *"He was more bashful about girls than anything else."*

And then came my favorite sentence about Oswald in the entire Warren Commission report: *"He was briefly a member of the Civil Air Patrol, and considered joining an organization of high school students interested in astronomy; occasionally he played pool or darts with his friend, Edward Voebel."*

Dave Ferrie? Carlos Marcello? Civil Air Patrol? Oh, I see, they played darts. And Oswald sort of dug astronomy. Good cold shoulder to these volunteer eyewitnesses, Earl Warren.

Dave Ferrie's name does not appear in Earl Warren's tedious index. Nor does Carlos Marcello's. In eight hundred eighty-eight pages of the single-volume official report that had been tasked to report the "truth" to the voters, there is no mention of Carlos Marcello or his pilot Dave Ferrie anywhere, not even playing darts. Not even Ferrie and Marcello sitting together in federal court defending the fraud charges over the fake Guatemalan birth certificate.

There was at least one more-than-suspicious coincidence involving the adult Oswald and Dave Ferrie that, had Oswald's interrogation not been interrupted on Sunday, Captain Fritz would have explored on Monday after the two eyewitnesses had come forward regarding Ferrie, Oswald, and the Civil Air Patrol. The coincidence is that Oswald's Communist Front, the pro-Castro "Fair Play for Cuba Committee," had its headquarters in the Camp Building in New Orleans. That's the same building where Dave Ferrie worked nearly every day, as part of the defense team helping Carlos Marcello with his legal woes regarding the fake Guatemalan birth certificate and Robert F. Kennedy's $850,000 tax lien.

There was another interesting coincidence that Captain Fritz would have explored with Oswald on Monday. This one involved Oswald and Carlos Marcello even more directly. When Oswald's father died of a heart attack when Oswald was four months old, Oswald was taken in to live with his uncle Charles "Dutz" Murret in New Orleans for four years. When Oswald returned from Russia in June 1962, Uncle Dutz had helped Oswald out financially. The coincidence is that Uncle Dutz was a professional bookmaker working for Carlos Marcello's New Orleans gambling operation.

Anything there worth following up, Chairman Warren?

Because of the two spontaneous witnesses' information, Dave Ferrie was taken in for questioning by the Secret Service that very Monday, November 25, 1963, a fact ignored by Chairman Warren. On his return from a weekend in Houston, Dave Ferrie told the Secret Service that after helping Carlos Marcello with his three-week fraudulent Guatemalan birth certificate trial in New Orleans resulting in an acquittal on the day of the John F. Kennedy assassination, Ferrie had taken a long weekend roller skating in Houston. Dave Ferrie admitted to the Secret Service that he previously had stated publicly that President John F. Kennedy should be shot for withdrawing air cover from the Bay of Pigs Invasion. Ferrie twice denied knowing or even so much as meeting Lee Harvey Oswald. And that lie was seemingly a safe lie with no chance of contradiction since Oswald had now been laid out dead for a day.

The authorities checked out Ferrie's plane and saw that it was in a messed-up condition—flat tires, missing instruments, not at all flyable. The condition of the plane was in the nature of an alibi. Of course, Marcello and Ferrie had no intention of flying Oswald anywhere, much less to a place where he could use that "Alek Hidell" fraudulent ID.

Dave Ferrie being picked up for questioning so quickly, routine in those days, no doubt made all the conspirators happy and proud that they had acted swiftly to give Oswald a Mafia "kiss."

Ferrie's lying about not ever meeting Oswald constitutes proof of his guilt in the assassination.

In the month before Marcello's trial for fraud, Ferrie had flown two trips totaling thirteen days to Guatemala to gather defense evidence for Marcello, whose ribs must have still hurt.

During the recruitment of Oswald to assassinate President Kennedy, the publicity of this trial would have made it easy to reassure a "lone cowboy" that Carlos Marcello was "big connected" in Guatemala, that a remote villa in Guatemala would be a good place in which to end up with his family and a suitcase full of American money.

"Interrogation interrupted" in Dallas left Captain Will Fritz with only one active murder case, an open-and-shut shooting on film of Oswald while the world watched. This was a case not worth Captain Fritz's time as an interrogator. Ruby had put an end to any future dogged detective work.

Had Oswald's interrogation not been interrupted by Jack Ruby, Captain Fritz would have had the opportunity to explore with Oswald the new material from the childhood friends linking the Kennedy brothers' enemy Carlos Marcello, through his pilot Dave Ferrie, to Lee Harvey Oswald. Let's not forget that Robert F. Kennedy, in addition to kidnapping him, knew Marcello and attempted to grill him before the Senate.

These two Civil Air Patrol witnesses linking Ferrie to Oswald, had Oswald not been silenced, would have created an invaluable line of questioning that easily would have shaken the truth out of Oswald. It was a line that formed beginning with Oswald's teenaged connection to Dave Ferrie, to the Camp Building, to Uncle Dutz working for Carlos Marcello, to Carlos Marcello's connection to Dave Ferrie, to Guatemala, to the "Alek Hidell" draft card useless in America, eventually leading to the two beeping patrolmen and to a con gameplan of an escorted escape to a safe house, and then on to a plan of an imaginary airstrip in Guatemala in an imaginary plane with the tempting promise of the final solution of the Oswalds' never-ending money problems.

Captain Fritz would have been able to plant seeds of a question in Oswald's mind one day and give them many days to grow.

Captain Fritz, examining the false draft card and tossing out "Guatemala" under his whispered breath, watching Oswald's body language, watching for him to stop breathing for an instant, where he placed his eyes when he lied, or to breathe faster, freeze, swallow, clench his jaw, yawn to hide his facial expression, or to stop blinking as a policeman often does when he lies, would have been instructive to Captain Fritz.

Fritz would have explored and exploited Oswald's feeling that he'd been a "patsy."

Fritz would have told Oswald that Officer J. D. Tippit had been in the airborne in World War II and had earned a Bronze Star when Russia and America were allies. Fritz would talk about Tippit and his family. Listening to the details, Oswald would be reminded that the case against him for killing Officer Tippit was going to lead to his execution. He might as well get back at those who caused him to do it, those who betrayed him and left him wandering in Oak Cliff "lonely as a cloud." No real man takes this mistreatment lying down, and he shouldn't either.

In 1978, fifteen years after the triple homicide in Dallas, Professor Blakey and his committee easily assembled five new eyewitnesses who had been in the New Orleans chapter of the Civil Air Patrol in 1955 with Oswald and Ferrie. These eyewitnesses testified that Dave Ferrie was their group leader and that a teenage Lee Harvey Oswald was in Ferrie's group. More than one said that Ferrie and Oswald spent time together.

Edward Voebel died in 1971, but had Earl Warren looked for these Civil Air Patrol witnesses in 1963 there would have been seven, at a minimum, including Voebel and the police informant. For sure, Chairman Warren was told of the existence of the police informant, Oswald's childhood friend Voebel, and the Civil Air Patrol connection with Ferrie. After all, the police and the Secret Service had promptly questioned them, and Warren was to inanely mention Voebel as a thrower of darts in his report. But Chairman Warren, using his methodology, deliberately suppressed the truth in all relevant areas and connections because Dave Ferrie would lead to Carlos Marcello, and Attorney General Robert F. Kennedy knew that led to CONTAC and that led to Ngo Dinh Diem and his brother Nhu.

In interrogating Oswald with this new information about his connection to Ferrie, Fritz would have nipped around the edges of a scenario that Ferrie was in on the assassination. With Ferrie in one room and Oswald in another, Fritz could have played one against the other. A dramatic example of that technique can be seen in Richard Brooks's film version of Truman Capote's true crime masterpiece *In Cold Blood* (Random House, 1965), published one year before the *Miranda* decision. Truman Capote testified before Congress against *Miranda*, telling Congress that the murders of *In Cold Blood* never would have been solved had *Miranda* been in existence during their investigation. But Earl Warren had taken *Miranda* out of the hands of Congress. Warren was to call all the shots of law enforcement forever.

In 1993, fifteen years after those five new Civil Air Patrol eyewitnesses had appeared for Professor Blakey, a photo surfaced on the PBS TV show *Frontline*. It is a candid shot of a 1955 Civil Air Patrol barbecue cookout in Dallas. It is plain to see that this is a small group, a club in which people know each other. There are nine men in the candid photo of young men grilling some food. A sixteen-year-old Cadet Lee Harvey Oswald is one, standing apart, looking more like a lonely cowboy than a "lone cowboy." Another is the grown man and group leader, Dave Ferrie.

Professor G. Robert Blakey's opinion that the Mafia killed Kennedy and got away with it was right as far as it went at the time. However, the professor was wrong about one thing: the Mafia *didn't* get away with it, thanks to the superb bulletproof laws inspired by Robert F. Kennedy that the great Professor Blakey had drafted; the unequaled heroism of Joe Pistone, as seen in *Donnie Brasco: Unfinished Business*; and the flair, knack, and bravery of those whom Blakey called the New Untouchables under Lin DeVecchio as portrayed in *We're Going to Win This Thing*.

Today we live in a land where organized crime fights over table scraps on its way out the door and something like "Dallas" never could happen again.

We did win this thing.

The New Untouchables and all their law enforcement partners, in and out of the Bureau, did it with intelligence, guts, and integrity.

As for the state of "Dallas" at this point, I quote the great Charlie Chan as played by Warner Oland in *Charlie Chan on Broadway*: *"Mud of bewilderment now beginning to clear from cool thought."*